.NDRA GUSTAFSON'S

C H E A P
E A T S

IN

PRAGUE VIENNA
BUDAPEST

SANDRA GUSTAFSON'S

CHEAP
EATS IN PRAGUE VIENNA BUDAPEST

**A Traveler's Guide to the
Best–Kept Secrets**

SANDRA A. GUSTAFSON

CHRONICLE BOOKS
SAN FRANCISCO

Printed in the United States of America.

ISBN 0-8118-2144-7
ISSN 1552-0907

Cover photograph: Dave Jacobs/Index Stock Imagery
Cover design: Yeong Sun-Park
Interior design: Words & Deeds
Maps: Ellen McElhinny

Distributed in Canada by
Raincoast Books
8680 Cambie Street
Vancouver, B.C. V6P 6M9

10 9 8 7 6 5 4 3 2 1

Chronicle Books
85 Second Street
San Francisco, CA 94105

www.chroniclebooks.com

To Kaye Adams, whose unfailing friendship, constant encouragement, and dedicated tactical support made this book possible.

Contents

To the Reader

Less than a century ago, the cities of Prague, Vienna, and Budapest belonged to the Austro-Hungarian Empire. Sharing many architectural, cultural, and culinary traits, they have been linked further by their distinct beauty and Old World charm, and they are today considered pivotal east-west crossroads in Europe. They are each the capital of their respective countries—namely, Czechoslovakia, Austria, and Hungary—and they each feature many of the same products in their cooking: game, fowl (both wild and tame), pork, sausages, freshwater fish, cabbage, beets, peppers, potatoes, onions, dumplings, pancakes, and heavy, dark, seeded breads, along with good wines and world-famous beers. Cooking methods and certain dishes are also similar, and on almost every menu you will find slow-cooked stews, goulash and creamy soups, fried and breaded meats, pickled vegetables, and rich pastries filled with fruit, cream, and poppyseeds. Despite their many similarities, however, each capital has its own unmistakable culinary character and unique food specialties—all of which you will find among the restaurants listed in this first edition of *Cheap Eats in Prague, Vienna, and Budapest*.

My purpose in writing this guide—as with all of the *Cheap Eats* guides—is not to provide a listing of the absolutely cheapest eats available. It is to give you a wide selection of all types of food choices that are the best value for the money in their category. In addition to serving good food at reasonable prices, the listings I recommend must also offer the type of atmosphere and ambiance that, whether grand or simple, has the potential to turn an everyday meal into a dining experience.

Though it perhaps should go without saying, I have been to every listing in this book—as well as to countless others that for one reason or another did not make the final cut—and I stand behind every selection. But I must caution you that in both Budapest and Prague the restaurant scene is evolving very rapidly, and you may encounter some changes in both management and pricing. If you do find certain restaurants different than they are described here, please let me know (see "Readers' Comments," page 168), as I follow up on every tip and letter.

During my *Cheap Eats* research trip of several months, I ate out three times a day, sampling the best and sometimes the worst food and service imaginable. I always arrived unexpected and, more importantly, uninvited, and I paid my own way. This enabled me not only to be objective about each restaurant but to receive the same quality of service and food you can expect when you go. My travels took me to all parts of these cities: from the most humble *klobásy* cart on Wenceslas Square in Prague to some of the finest restaurants in Vienna—serving heavenly *Wiener Schnitzel* and *Apfelstrudel*—to homey Budapest lunch rooms dishing out robust goulash soups.

Wherever your dining path may lead you in any of these beautiful cities, I hope that *Cheap Eats* enables you to enjoy the culinary delights of the local cuisines and to leave with pleasant memories of many satisfying meals. I wish you *Dobrou chut'! Guten Appetit!* and *Jó étvágyat!*

How to Use Cheap Eats in Prague, Vienna, and Budapest

Each listing in *Cheap Eats in Prague, Vienna, and Budapest* includes the following information: the name and address of the establishment; the area of the city in which it is located; the telephone number; the closest underground transportation stop; the days it is open and closed; annual closing dates, if any; hours of service; whether reservations are necessary; credit cards accepted; the average price of a three-course à la carte meal without beverages; descriptions and prices for fixed-price meals, if served; what the cover and service charges are; and if English is spoken and/or if there is a menu in English. Nonsmoking establishments, or those with a nonsmoking section, are also noted. The number in parenthesis to the left of each *Cheap Eats* entry indicates its number as it appears on the appropriate city map. A dollar sign ($) to the right of an entry means it is a Big Splurge.

The following abbreviations are used to indicate which credit cards are accepted:

American Express	AE
Diners Club	DC
MasterCard or Access	MC
Visa	V

At the end of each city's restaurant listings is a glossary of useful phrases and menu terms. These glossaries are not intended to be comprehensive. Their purpose is to help you negotiate simple courtesies, to help you read the different menus, and to introduce you to some of the basic food terms. At the very end of the book is a page for your comments and an address to write to me about your experiences in using this book. I cannot emphasize enough how important your reactions are to me, and I can assure you that I follow up on every compliment or complaint.

Important Telephone Notice for Prague and Budapest

Currently, the telephone systems in both Czechoslovakia and Hungary are being privatized, and this means—much to the dismay of visitors, residents, and travel writers—that the telephone numbering systems in both Prague and Budapest have been and will be changing. Unfortunately, the phone numbers are being changed piecemeal over an extended period of time, and no one seems to know when the process will be complete. Equally upsetting is that the automated system for keeping track of the changes—and that tells you the new number when you dial the old number—is extremely limited and can't be relied upon by the visitor.

If you are calling from the United States and you dial a number that's no longer working, you should dial 00 and ask for international directory assistance. This operator will connect you with an English-speaking operator in the foreign city you are trying to reach. If you are calling from within either Prague or Budapest, ask your hotel desk clerk to assist you. He or she will be able to negotiate the phone system more efficiently and may have access to the most up-to-date information.

The phone numbers given with each *Cheap Eats* listing have been rechecked and were correct at press time, but you can be almost assured that some will have changed by your arrival. For their help in verifying telephone numbers, I would like to thank Philip Zvonicek at the Embassy of the Czech Republic in Washington, D.C., for his help with Prague and Tünde Varga for her help with Budapest.

PRAGUE

What a difference a decade—and a revolution—can make. When I lived in Prague in the early 1980s, there were few restaurants and no good ones. Bureaucratic Communist zealots kept check on all aspects of life, including culinary matters. Officials required every new dish offered on any menu to undergo testing at the Ministry of Health before being presented to the public. Rather than wade through the morass of red tape involved, restaurants continued serving meals that were already approved and listed in three state-issued books, whose scintillating titles were *Recipes for Warm Meals* and *Recipes for Cold Meals, Volumes I and II.* No wonder no one ever ate out!

Although the Velvet Revolution of 1989 was a quick and successful one, the food revolution hasn't kept pace. Today, even with over two thousand restaurants, Prague is still a city more noteworthy for its beauty than its cuisine. However, things *are* changing, and relatively quickly: the restaurant industry has been taken out of government control and become privatized, and new places are bursting on the scene, making flashy debuts and fleeting loyalties. But you will find that old habits die hard, and some restaurants are still stuck in the noncompetitive Socialistic mentality of the past. Cheap Eaters in Prague must therefore be forgiving, realizing that while owners are struggling to cope in a competitive society, food and service can be uneven—more often than not in the same restaurant on successive nights.

To enjoy Czech food, you must put aside concerns over expanding waistlines: this heavy fare is loaded with fat, sugar, starch, and cream. The traditional Czech troika of *vepřové, knedlíky,* and *zelí*—pork, dumplings, and cabbage—still reigns supreme, as do the everpresent *palačinky*—dessert pancakes filled with fruit, ice cream, chocolate, and whipped cream. Diners will also find preparations of wild game and fowl, carp and trout from the lakes in southern Bohemia, Prague ham, spicy sausages, and robust soups. Pizza is everywhere, as are Big Macs and buckets of Kentucky Fried Chicken.

This section on Prague is divided into the major areas of the city where most visitors will be. Wherever you eat in Prague, remember to have patience and understand that things are changing at a breakneck pace. Keep your expectations realistic and you are bound to have many good Cheap Eats in Prague. I wish you *Dobrou chut'*.

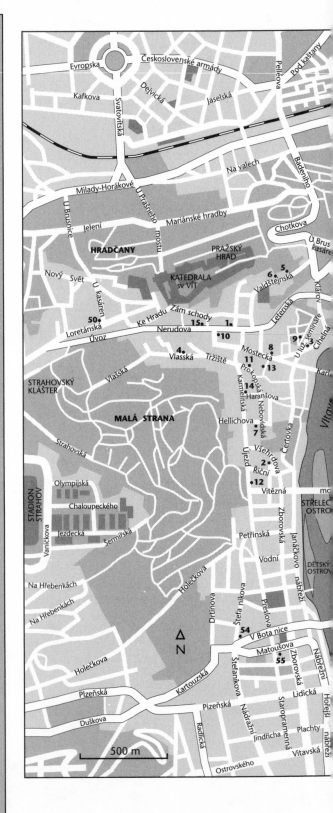

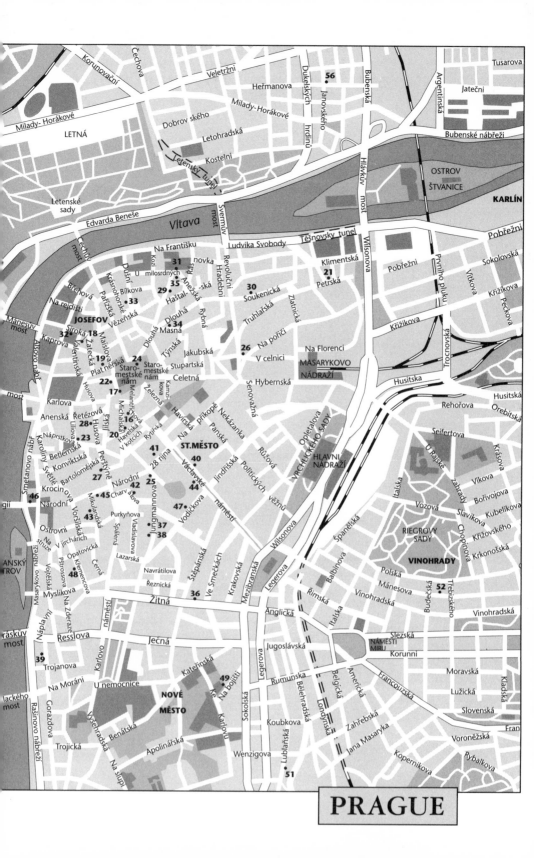

PRAGUE

Cheap Eating Tips in Prague

1. The Czechs tend to eat early, and many small Cheap Eating establishments do not prepare their daily specials in bulk. For best selection, go early for lunch and don't expect much after 9 P.M.

2. Communal dining is normal, especially in inexpensive restaurants, so be prepared to share your table and wish your fellow diners *Dobrou chut'!*

3. Dining in Prague is inexpensive in comparison to other major Western European capital cities, therefore you can have more elaborate meals in nicer restaurants and still stay within a modest budget.

4. On the other hand, Czech cuisine has not reached world-class status, so be prepared to experience food ranging from good to indifferent on all price levels.

5. You must be forgiving about the service. It can be good, but all too often surly waiters still unaccustomed to a capitalist work ethic ignore diners almost to the point where one feels as though they are taking root between courses.

6. Unfortunately, many waiters consider bill padding not just a perk but an entitlement of their job. Bosses tend to look the other way, since many may be in on the take. For a detailed discussion of how to avoid being ripped off, see "Paying the Bill," page 20.

7. Tipping is not mandatory, but unless the service and/or the meal is really terrible, round off the total and give a little extra. If you were especially pleased, leave 10 percent.

8. Know how much you are spending for everything you consume. Ask about that bowl of nuts on the table, as it can be a bill inflater; some places even calculate the cost per nut! Also, if you change the garnish on your dish from fried to boiled potatoes, you could be charged a supplement equal to the price of the dish in its entirety.

9. Most restaurants have multilingual menus that try to cover all the culinary bases. Don't be fooled, since this is impossible to do well. To avoid disappointment, ask for the daily specials, which may be listed in Czech. They will at least be freshly prepared, not dragged from the deep freeze.

10. Reservations are always preferred, and they are almost mandatory in better places. However, unless your Czech is very good, ask your hotel to make your reservations. This way the restaurant will have to answer to the hotel and risk losing further business if the service is poor or they try to cheat you.

General Information about Cheap Eating in Prague

Prague still seems, after many rival cities, one of the most beautiful in all the world.

—Anonymous

Where to Eat

The most obvious destination for a sit-down meal is a *restaurace*, or restaurant, where you will be served at a table and expected to order more than just a salad and a glass of mineral water. *Vinárny*, or wine bars, can be anything from a little five-seat spot dispensing local wines to something quite pricey with food and wine in the Big Splurge category. A beer joint or beer hall is called either a *pivnice, hostinec,* or *hospoda.* Here, food is an afterthought to keep the customers sober enough to continue ordering more *pivo* (beer). Cafés usually serve a hot meal at lunch, but seldom at dinner, though throughout the day you can order sandwiches, pastries, and ice cream desserts. There are also stand-up *bufets,* self-service cafeterias, and *lahudkys,* where sandwiches are dispensed. Finally, the Cheapest Eat of all can often be found at one of the sausage wagons that seem to be everywhere, especially along Wenceslas Square.

What to Eat

Czech food does not attempt to speak to the gourmet diner well-versed in fine preparations. It does speak to those who appreciate sturdy stick-to-your ribs food that takes well to frying and stewing. Imagination and presentation are not high on the lists of many current Prague chefs. That is the bad news. The good news is that all that is changing . . . and for the better.

Generally Czech restaurant menus have two types of main courses: a ready-to-serve *hotová jídla* and a cooked-to-order *minutky.* The ready-to-serve meals are usually meats cooked in sauces or stews and served with potatoes and dumplings—*knedlíky*—to soak up the juices, and the cooked-to-order dishes consist of grilled meat and fish. Dumplings come many ways: a floury *mouka knedlíky,* the mashed potato version (*bramborová knedlíky*), and the *špekové knedlíky,* made with bacon. Dessert dumplings surround pieces of stewed fruit and are just like lead balls. Fresh vegetables are gaining a small toe-hold, but they are still the exception rather than the rule. Cabbage, potatoes, and the occasional carrot are cooked fresh, and tomatoes and cucumbers are good, but forget everything else. The asparagus that appears on many menus is usually canned; corn is frozen, as are green beans.

Sausage lovers are in heaven among the many street vendors that dot the city. Never mind the nutritional value, which is about nil, unless saturated fat is an integral part of your daily diet. The hot dog look-a-like *liberečky párky* and the *cabajka*—flavored with paprika—are popular varieties. If you want a chicken or beef dog, ask for *drůbeží párky* or a *hovězí párky*. Vegetarians can try the *bramborák,* a minced potato pancake flavored with garlic and marjoram, deep-fat fried, and zapped in the microwave on order. If it's crisp, it's fresh. If it folds in half, it has been around for awhile. Finally, there is *langoše,* a popular street snack virtually devoid of nutritional merit and guaranteed to send health foodies running in terror. It is a hunk of raw dough that's deep fried and covered in garlic, ketchup, or cheese (or all three) and consumed while the fat drips off your chin.

Surprisingly popular, and reasonably healthy besides, are dishes featuring carp and fresh trout. Eel is also available. For a nourishing winter lunch, it is hard to beat a bowl of hearty Czech soup and a slice or two of dark bread. However, a word of caution for the uninitiated: there are some varieties you may want to avoid. *Drst'ková,* a favorite, has cooked pieces of cow's stomach floating on top, and *zabijáčková polévka*'s main ingredient is pig's blood.

Believe it or not, vegetarians are not out in the cold in Prague. On most menus is *smažený sýr,* cheese that has been breaded and fried and usually served with tartar sauce and a little salad. Fresh cauliflower and mushrooms are also served in this way. Omelettes are easy to find, and so are dumplings chopped up and fried in an egg batter. Many places offer a vegetable gratin, meatless pastas, and even vegetable plates, but the variety and quality on these is sometimes limited.

For dessert? Well, it's usually a short list comprised of *palačinky,* oversized pancakes filled with ice cream and fruit and topped with chocolate sauce and whipped cream; anything with a banana on it (thanks to the years the Czechs went without bananas); and some unremarkable cakes layered with cream and fruit.

For a detailed glossary of menu terms, see page 62.

What to Drink

While Czech food may not rate rave reviews, no one can say that about the beer, which is considered the finest in the world. The Czechs call their beer "liquid bread," or *tekutý chléb,* and consider it like a food—which is not surprising when you consider that the average Czech citizen consumes almost three hundred pints of beer a year, making one in every five citizens a registered alcoholic. Pilsener Urquell from the town of Plzeň is thought by many to be the best Czech beer. The clear, amber lager was first brewed there in 1842, and it continues to be made there today using the same fermentation process. In Tokyo it is sold for more than $10; in Prague, for less than a dollar. Not far behind in popularity is the original Budweiser, brewed in Česke Budějovice.

To order your *pivo,* say *pivo, prosím,* and you will get a half litre of light beer. If you want a smaller glass, say *malé pivo,* or if you like your beer dark, say *černé pivo, prosím.* The waiter will come around with more beer unless you tell him not to by placing the beer mat on top of your glass. Wherever you happen to be drinking, the Czech toast is *Na zdraví!*

Czech wine is a distant second to beer. Best bets come from Moravia, with the white being slightly less rough than the red. From September on, *burčák,* the Czech version of Beaujolais Nouveau, is popular, but watch out—what goes down like velvet in the evening hits hard as a hammer in the morning.

Absinthe is illegal almost worldwide, but in Prague you can find it in many places that serve liquid refreshment. Made from fermented wormwood, it is a powerful elixir that has frightening side effects, such as hallucinations, seizures, and amnesia. It has also been said to deworm intestines, kill fleas, and provide eternal youth. Taste descriptions range from "toxic waste" at its worst to "bilge water" at its best. When drinking it, certain steps must be followed. A spoonful of absinthe-soaked sugar is lighted and allowed to caramelize and liquefy, and then it is stirred into a glass of water and absinthe and consumed. After that, you are on your own with the consequences.

Other native drinks include Becherovka, whose twenty-herb recipe is so highly acclaimed that ten million bottles of the stuff are sold yearly, and it's found in every bar in Prague. It is made in Karlovy Vary and said to calm stomach distress. Also popular, but without medicinal properties, are Slivovice (plum brandy) from Slovakia and Borovicka, made from juniper berries.

Finally, there is coffee. You can find espresso, cappuccino, and filtered coffee all over Prague. If you are not careful, you may also get *turecká,* a strong Turkish brew with the grounds still floating in the cup when it is served. If you like this sort of caffeine fix, add a cube of sugar to cut the heavy taste, and wait a few minutes for the grounds to settle before taking your first sip.

Reservations

Are reservations necessary? Not in beer halls or cafés, but in better places a two- or three-day notice is often required. If your Czech is limited, ask your hotel to reserve for you. This should definitely give you the edge if the service or food are not up to par. At least the restaurant will have to answer to the hotel, and risk the loss of future business, if they do not treat guests correctly.

Paying the Bill and Tipping

All *Cheap Eats in Prague* listings state whether credit cards are accepted, and if so, which ones. The concept of plastic money is just now catching on in Prague, so many more restaurants will be accepting them in the future.

Each listing also tells you if there is a cover charge, and if so, how much it will be per person, and it tells you the establishment's policy regarding the service charge (which is the same as the tip). Many include a service charge in the price of your meal, a few add a service charge onto your total bill (10 to 15 percent), some don't include a service charge but still expect you to leave a tip of 10 to 15 percent, and some don't include a service charge and don't expect any gratuity. All these differences can be confusing, and each listing in *Cheap Eats* tells you exactly what to expect. Here is a list of the terms that are used:

Service included: This means a restaurant has included the service charge (a government-allowed 23 percent VAT) in the price of your food and drink. This amount will not appear as an extra charge on your bill. Even when service is included, it is customary to round up the total of your bill as a small extra gratuity if you were happy with the service.

_____% *service added to your bill:* This indicates that the restaurant will automatically add a service charge onto your bill at the stated percentage, and you are not expected to leave anything more.

Service discretionary: This means no service charge is added to or included in your bill, but the restaurant does expect a tip of 10 or 15 percent.

No service charged or expected: Even when no tip is expected, rounding up the total of your bill is a polite gesture if you were happy with the service.

Your bill will be presented in one of two ways: In cheaper places, the waiter will usually keep a running total on a piece of paper at your table. When you are ready to pay, signal the person with the black wallet, not your waiter, and state the amount you are paying in total—not how much change you want back. In other restaurants, you will be presented the bill in the normal fashion.

Restaurant bill padding and downright cheating is rampant in Prague. It has been said that 3 percent of some restaurants' income comes from this despicable activity. Be particularly wary of restaurants adding a service charge onto your bill when it has already been included in the price of the meal. To avoid massive ripoffs, follow these suggestions.

1. Ask the price of everything you are eating, from the bowl of nuts (which might be charged per nut) on the table when you sit down to the tray of tempting appetizers passed as you are ordering, to the last drop of dessert and coffee you consume. If you change the garnishes, or redesign any part of what you order, the changes could cost you as much as the price of the original dish.

2. When presented with the bill, scrutinize every mark on it and question anything you do not understand. Do not be pressured to rush in doing this.

3. If paying by credit card, write the amount in letters (such as, twenty-seven Kč. Draw a line through every blank square on the receipt, and tip in cash. Don't forget the receipt.

4. Remember that tipping is not mandatory, and one should be left only if the service was good. Waiters are not well paid, so rounding off the bill is always appreciated. If the waiter did something special for you, leave 10 percent extra.

Holidays

Many shops and museums and all banks are closed on holidays. Restaurants say they are always open, but often at the last minute smaller ones will decide to close. Most of the larger establishments are open year-round, closing only for Christmas and New Year's, but to avoid disappointment, call to check.

January 1	New Year's Day
Easter Sunday and Monday	Dates vary
May 1	Labor Day
May 8	Liberation Day
July 5	Cyril and Methodius Day
July 6	Jan Hus Day
October 28	Independence Day
December 24–26	Christmas

Finding an Address

Finding an address in Prague is not difficult, but you will notice that each building has two numbers, a red one and a blue one. The blue number is the street address. The red number is a city registry number for the building, and you don't need to worry about it.

Transportation

All the *Cheap Eats in Prague* listings give the nearest underground metro stop and the letter of the line it's on (either line A, B, or C). The public transportation system is very good and simple to use, and you should not hesitate to ride on it.

Conversely, taxis should be avoided at almost all costs. The head of the taxi union in Prague has admitted that many cabbies wire their seats so that by pressing a button they can zap troublesome passengers with electric jolts. It is a given that foreigners will be overcharged and pay more than local Czechs for the same ride. To avoid the worst of taxi thievery, follow these guidelines.

1. Make sure you are getting into an authorized taxi, which has a registration number, fares clearly printed on the doors, and a black-and-white checkered stripe along the side.

2. Drivers are supposed to use their meters, and when they do there will be an initial amount shown, around 12Kč. Watch that they don't switch from fare type 1 to 2, which is the most expensive fare and applies outside Prague's city limits. The rate set at 1 should not be more than 16Kč per kilometer. At the end of the ride, the driver is required to give you a receipt—an *ucet* or *paragon*. Few do this unless asked. The honest ones will print one out on the machine attached to the meter. Slick ones will write yours on a piece of paper.

3. Ask your hotel to call a cab, and find out what a reasonable fare should be to your destination. Do not get into the taxi without discussing the fare in advance, and still insist that the meter be used.

4. If you hail a cab on the street, you can almost count on getting gouged.

5. At the airport, use only a taxi where a dispatcher is present, and discuss the price before getting into the cab or putting your luggage in the trunk.

Important Telephone Notice

The telephone system in Czechoslovakia is being privatized. This means that although the telephone numbers for the listings in this section were correct at press time, they may have changed by your arrival. If you are calling from the United States and you dial a number that's no longer working, dial 00 and ask for international directory assistance. The operator will connect you with an English-speaking operator in Prague. If you are calling from Prague, ask your hotel desk clerk to assist you. He or she may have access to the most up-to-date information.

Restaurants in Prague by Area

MALÁ STRANA (LESSER TOWN) ────────────

Malá Strana, which means the Little Quarter or Lesser Town, dates from the thirteenth century, and it's on the west bank of the River Vltava. Dominated by St. Nicholas Church, a Jesuit basilica that took seventy-five years to build, Malá Strana is one of Prague's most picturesque quarters, where you will find Baroque churches, monumental palaces, and embassy residences mixed with narrow winding streets, hidden gardens, brightly painted houses, and many shops and restaurants geared toward visitors and locals with money.

RESTAURANTS

(1)	Avalon Bar & Grill	24
(2)	Bar Bar	24
(3)	Čertovka $	25
(4)	Lobkovická Vinárna $	25
(5)	Pálffy Palác	26
(6)	Restaurant u Kolowrata $	27
(7)	U Modré Kachničky $	27
(8)	U Sněděného Krámu	28
(9)	U Tří Pštrosů $	28
(10)	U Tří Zlatých Hvězd $	29
(11)	Vinárna u Maltézských Rytířů $	30

CAFÉS

(12)	Café Savoy	30
(13)	Chiméra Galerie-Café	31
(14)	Petarství V Karmelitské	31

PUBS

(15)	U Kocoura	32

A dollar sign ($) indicates a Big Splurge.

Restaurants

(1) AVALON BAR & GRILL
Malostranské náměstí 12, Prague 1

TELEPHONE
530 276, 530 236

METRO
A, Malostranská

OPEN
Daily

CLOSED
Never

HOURS
11 A.M.–1 A.M., continuous service; Sun brunch 11 A.M.–4 P.M.; jazz, Tues, Fri, Sat, 8–11 P.M., Sun noon–3 P.M.

RESERVATIONS
Suggested

CREDIT CARDS
AE, MC, V

À LA CARTE
225–450Kč, from sandwich to 3-course meal

FIXED-PRICE MENU
Sun brunch, 350Kč, 3 courses, with unlimited nonalcoholic drinks

SERVICE
No service charged or expected

ENGLISH
Yes, and menu in English

Think southern California yuppie bar and grill and you have the Avalon pegged. Prints of old American cars vie for space with a collection of motorcycle photos in the second room by the bar. Along with fresh flowers, a palm tree or two, and a friendly waitstaff clad in Levis, it creates a casual and relaxed atmosphere for a snack or a full meal.

The menu is as California inspired as the decor. For something light, order a feta quesadilla with pesto, salmon and spinach quiche, or chili-rubbed, charred beef carpaccio with a garlic confit. Also on board are hamburgers, club sandwiches, pastas, soups, and large salads. Main courses include lamb chops served with fresh vegetables and roasted potatoes, fish and chips (cod soaked in a beer batter and served with fried potatoes), grilled fish, and a blowout barbeque plate with a chicken leg, pork chop, and beef tenderloin. Still hungry? Go for the chocolate brownie with ice cream or the rich banana and kahlua chocolate mousse cake.

NOTE: Don't make the mistake of eating downstairs in the sister restaurant—the CircleLine Brasserie—which has very good food but is not in the spirit of a Cheap Eat in Prague.

(2) BAR BAR
Všehrdova 17, Prague 1

TELEPHONE
532 941

METRO
A, Malostranská

OPEN
Daily

CLOSED
Never

HOURS
Mon–Fri 11 A.M.–midnight, Sat–Sun noon–midnight

RESERVATIONS
Not necessary

CREDIT CARDS
MC, V

À LA CARTE
Salads 60–100Kč, crêpes 50–150Kč, grilled meats 90–250Kč

Locals are common and tourists rare at Daniela Vejvodova's Bar Bar, thanks to its location just far enough away from action central to keep it honest and real. When you arrive, you must *push* the door very hard. The first two times I tried to eat here, I thought the door was locked and the restaurant closed.

As you enter the basement location, you are met with an assortment of what must be the world's ugliest men's neckties and a rocking horse on the landing; downstairs in the main section, decorations include a few antiques displayed under the windows, a bird mobile, and an old radio. Seating is around bare wooden bistro tables. The menu starts with a few sandwiches and some main-course salads, a daily soup, and grilled meats. Ignore all this and go right for their specialty, *palačinky,* the Czech

version of French crêpes. There are a dozen savory possibilities named after European cities or monuments, and
as many sweet dessert crêpes, most of which feature fruit
combinations with liqueurs. The chef is accommodating
if you don't see the exact combination you want.

(3) ČERTOVKA $
U Lužického semináře 24/100, Prague 1

Location, location, location . . . Čertovka has it in
spades. The restaurant occupies a platinum location on
the River Vltava with a view of the Charles Bridge.
Centuries ago, this section of the river was once used by
mills. The building dates to the early 1600s, when it
housed a leather crafts shop.

If you are here in the winter, reserve a window table
in the more formal dining room upstairs. In the summer
you definitely want to be downstairs, sitting at one of
the umbrella-shaded tables that overlook the river and
the white swans and ducks paddling by. With the lights
of the Charles Bridge and Prague Castle beyond, it is
truly a romantic slice of heaven. Because reservations are
not accepted for the terrace, plan to arrive early rather
than during peak meal times. Another bonus of the
outside area and the *vinárna* beside it is the menu. It is
less expensive than the one upstairs, but all the food
comes out of the same kitchen. The dishes are international in scope and provide no surprises. Selections vary
from the Charles IV cold meat platter—with enough
pork and smoked meat for two to share nicely—to omelettes and sirloin steaks.

(4) LOBKOVICKÁ VINÁRNA $
Vlašská 17, Prague 1

The Lobkovická Vinárna is an elegant choice if you
want to dress your best and celebrate a special occasion
in Prague. The wine tavern began more than three centuries ago as the place where the princes from the
Lobkowicz family sold the wine made at their Castle
Mělník, located just outside of Prague on the Rivers
Elbe and Moldau. Today it is owned and run by George
and Bettina Lobkowicz of the same aristocratic family.

The dramatic interior consists of a series of beautiful
rooms decorated with lush orange walls and black-and-
white-stripe upholstery on comfortable high-back chairs
and settees. Table settings are just as formal, and so are

FIXED-PRICE MENU
None

SERVICE
No service charged or expected

ENGLISH
Yes, and menu in English

TELEPHONE
538 853

METRO
A, Malostranská

OPEN
Daily

CLOSED
3 weeks in March, dates vary

HOURS
11:30 A.M.–11:30 P.M.,
continuous service (sometimes
closed earlier in the winter)

RESERVATIONS
Essential in the summer, but
not accepted for garden tables

CREDIT CARDS
AE, DC, MC, V

À LA CARTE
Upstairs, 400–500Kč;
downstairs and terrace, 200–
350Kč

FIXED-PRICE MENU
None

SERVICE
35Kč cover, service discretionary

ENGLISH
Yes, and menu in English

TELEPHONE
530 185

METRO
A, Malostranská

OPEN
Mon–Sat

CLOSED
Sun, 3 weeks in January

HOURS
Lunch noon–3 P.M., dinner 6
P.M.–midnight

RESERVATIONS
Advised

CREDIT CARDS
AE, MC, V

À LA CARTE
600–1000Kč

FIXED-PRICE MENU
None

SERVICE
40Kč cover, service included

ENGLISH
Yes, and menu in English

the tuxedoed waiters. The food keeps pace with the surroundings. When you are seated, you will be served a venison pâté garnished with cranberry sauce and a basket of bread and butter. The menu changes with the seasons, and it offers admirable preparations of wild game, fresh fish, and all the meats. If you like duck, consider the whole roast duck served in its own roasting pan, garnished with potato dumplings and red and white cabbage. Beef eaters will be happy with the chateaubriand or the beefsteak Lobkowicz, which is topped with ham and surrounded in a white wine mushroom sauce. For dessert? The hands-down winner in my book is the chocolate fondue with fresh fruit for dipping. Your wine will be an excellent bottle from the cellars of the family castle.

NOTE: The Castle Lobkowicz, situated in Mělník about twenty-five miles from Prague, is open to the public. Guests can visit the art collection or enjoy wine tasting in the fourteenth-century wine cellar. There is also a wine bar in the castle vaults and a restaurant with views of the rivers.

(5) PÁLFFY PALÁC
Valdštejnská 14, Prague 1

TELEPHONE
513 2418, 5732 0570

METRO
A, Malostranská

OPEN
Daily

CLOSED
Major holidays

HOURS
11 A.M.–11 P.M., continuous service; fixed-price lunch Mon–Fri 11 A.M.–5 P.M.; Sat and Sun brunch 11 A.M.–3 P.M.

RESERVATIONS
Advised, especially in the summer

CREDIT CARDS
AE, MC, V

À LA CARTE
Lunch or dinner 550–750Kč

FIXED-PRICE MENU
Lunch 380Kč, 4 courses, including wine or beer; weekend brunch, set prices for starters 120Kč, main courses 160Kč, desserts 110Kč, drinks 80Kč

For Cheap Eats at the Pálffy Palác, come for the fixed-price lunch between 11 A.M. and 5 P.M. during the week, or for brunch on Saturday and Sunday—but *never* for dinner. For both lunch and dinner, diners have the same daily changing meal choices, but at lunch you get a glass of wine or beer with a four-course meal that costs about half of what dinner will be. Fellow lunch diners will be students from the music conservatory who are paying in the neighborhood of 60Kč for their lunch and using paper napkins. You will be seated in the same grand Baroque room at a properly set table graced by either fresh flowers or a bowl of fresh fruit. During warm weather, you can sit on the terrace with a corner view of the Prague Castle. Though the menu reads better than the food sometimes tastes—the fish is frozen and the cooking can be uneven—on a warm day, you can't fault the setting.

The four-course, fixed-price midday meal might include pastry-wrapped snails in garlic sauce, vegetable soup with parmesan toast, rabbit, grilled salmon, fresh vegetables, and tiramisu or cheesecake. On Saturday or Sunday, it is easy to eat à la carte and not spend a fortune.

For example, you could graze through starters of caviar with butter and toast, shrimp and avocado salad, or have a hot cinnamon hazelnut raisin roll served with honey cream. Main courses include three filled croissants, several crêpes, omelettes, and baked brie served with rosemary and garlic roasted potatoes. To go with the meal, order a Bloody Mary, mimosa, screwdriver, or homemade hot chocolate.

SERVICE
30Kč cover at dinner, service included lunch and dinner

ENGLISH
Yes, and menu in English

(6) RESTAURANT U KOLOWRATA $
Valdšejnská 18, Prague 1

U Kolowrata is an ornately decorated restaurant on Wallenstein Square. The lavish blue hand-painted interior depicts Czech guilds, crafts, and artisans from the 1600s. While it is too bright for much hand-holding intimacy, the room has a feel of quiet and calmness that is missing in many Prague restaurants. Businesspeople at lunchtime and well-dressed locals in the evenings keep this respected place fully booked while others in the area are standing empty. The traditional service is always correct and usually slow, so this is not the place to go if you have somewhere else to be later.

The food offers a good selection of recognizable international standards and Czech dishes that are well executed and nicely presented. I like to begin with the creamy potato mushroom soup or the baked chèvre, served on toast with walnuts and honey. The rabbit cooked with onion and bacon is an interesting choice, and so is the roasted pike-perch with almonds. For dessert order the crème caramel gilded with whipped cream.

TELEPHONE
531 546

METRO
A, Malostranská

OPEN
Daily

CLOSED
Never

HOURS
11:30 A.M.–11 P.M., continuous service

RESERVATIONS
Essential for dinner

CREDIT CARDS
AE, MC, V

À LA CARTE
600–750Kč

FIXED-PRICE MENU
None

SERVICE
25Kč cover, service included

ENGLISH
Yes, and menu in English

(7) U MODRÉ KACHNIČKY $
Nebovidská 6, Prague 1

Everyone from prime ministers and presidents to Tom Cruise and Madeleine Albright have eaten at U Modré Kachničky (The Blue Duckling). Located in a bright blue corner building on a little backwater street in picturesque Malá Strana, the restaurant opened in 1993 and has been a success from the get-go. There are only forty-five places set in three charmingly furnished small rooms with Oriental rugs scattered on tile floors, hand-painted walls hung with framed prints and mirrors, and a wonderful old ceramic heater in the back room. It all adds up to be one of the most intimate and stylish restaurants in Prague.

TELEPHONE
0602 3535 59, 2732 0308

METRO
A, Malostranská

OPEN
Daily

CLOSED
2 days at Christmas

HOURS
Lunch noon–4 P.M., dinner 6:30–11:30 P.M.

RESERVATIONS
Essential; for dinner, 2–3 days ahead

CREDIT CARDS
AE

The food is aimed at carnivores who love duck, pheasant, wild boar, venison, and steaks. Duck is fixed four ways: domestic duck comes with dumplings and cabbage, with apples and croquettes, or with paprika rice and bacon, and wild duck comes with an orange sauce. The rabbit is roasted with garlic and onions and served with spinach and dumplings. The Malá Strana Templars' Sword is a meat-eating feast prepared for two, made up of flambéed beef, pork tenderloin, ham, liver, bacon, onions, and boiled potatoes. Even though the main courses are garnished, you should have one order of their mushroom and cheese risotto to share. The high calorie count doesn't stop with dessert, especially not with the *palačinky*—pancakes filled with fresh fruit, ice cream, and whipped cream.

À LA CARTE
600–700Kč
FIXED-PRICE MENU
None
SERVICE
Service included
ENGLISH
Yes, and menu in English

(8) U SNĚDENÉHO KRÁMU
Mostecká 5, Prague 1

TELEPHONE
531 795
METRO
A, Malostranská
OPEN
Daily
CLOSED
Never
HOURS
Noon–11 P.M., continuous service
RESERVATIONS
Not necessary
CREDIT CARDS
AE, MC, V
À LA CARTE
300–450Kč
FIXED-PRICE MENU
200Kč, 3 courses, no choices, beverage extra
SERVICE
No service charged or expected
ENGLISH
Yes, and menu in English

There is lots to recommend about U Sněděného Krámu besides the dynamite location near the Malá Strana end of the Charles Bridge and the Cheap Eater–friendly fixed-price meal, which is available anytime. This turn-of-the-century beer house is named after a famous 1930s Czech tragicomedic film, photos of which hang around the bar. The water fountain at the base of the spiral staircase used to be on the outside of the building for residents to wash their hands. Other decorative touches include musical instruments, boots, and a clock dangling from the ceiling, as well as old Prague photos, two antique typewriters, and vintage accordions. The booth–bench seating blends in well with the eclectic atmosphere. Word has it that Václav Havel eats here, along with twenty bodyguards. I didn't see him when I was there, but I did see plenty of locals and visitors filling the place. The fixed-price meal changes daily and offers a soup, main course, and dessert. One day it might be tomato soup, roast duck, and a sweet pancake; the next, potato soup, a pork dish, and ice cream. Four Bohemian beers are poured: Pilsner, Budweiser-Budvar, Gambrinus, and dark Purkmistr.

(9) U TŘÍ PŠTROSŮ $
Dražického náměstí 12, Prague 1

TELEPHONE
5732 0565
METRO
A, Malostranská
OPEN
Daily

For centuries, U Tří Pštrosů (The Three Ostriches) has occupied a prime corner of Prague real estate at the end of the Charles Bridge. During the Communist-dominated era in Prague, the small hotel and restaurant were considered to be the most charming address in town; however, since the Velvet Revolution, it has met some very serious competition. One cannot dispute the dramatic setting—almost in the shade of the famous bridge—but the food is another thing. I think any restaurant that peddles a tired menu still listing canned fruits for dessert is suspect. In a cafeteria it might be acceptable, but not in a restaurant with these prices. Cheap Eaters should skip the restaurant (which is a not-worth-it Big Splurge) and stop by the snack bar instead for a coffee or light snack when strolling across the Charles Bridge.

CLOSED
Never

HOURS
Snack bar 11 A.M.–7 P.M.; in restaurant, stated hours are noon–11 P.M., but in fact hot meals are only noon–2 P.M. for lunch and 6–10 P.M. for dinner

RESERVATIONS
Suggested in the restaurant

CREDIT CARDS
AE, MC, V

À LA CARTE
Restaurant, 500Kč; snack bar, sandwiches from 60Kč, sweets from 20Kč

FIXED-PRICE MENU
None

SERVICE
25Kč cover in restaurant only; service included in restaurant and snack bar

ENGLISH
Yes, and menu in English

(10) U TŘÍ ZLATÝCH HVĚZD $
Malostranské náměstí 8/263, Prague 1

The "Three Golden Stars" is in a three-hundred-year-old building under the arches facing the Church of St. Nicholas, a monumental Baroque church built by the Jesuits between 1703 and 1755. The best seats are at one of the eight tables upstairs in a room with frescoed walls, comfortable upholstered chairs, and pink linens. Come for the fixed-price menus between 11:30 A.M. and 5 P.M. and you will have a Cheap Eat in lovely surroundings. Eat later, and without careful selection, prices can climb into the Big Splurge category.

The two fixed-price menus may change their offerings, but you will always have good food and value for your money. With the less expensive one, you could start with a pâté, followed by beef in a cream sauce and accompanied by dumplings, and end with cranberries with apple pie or cake for dessert. Spend a little more and you might begin with a soup, followed by pork steak with rice flavored with bacon, mushrooms, and onions, and have your apple pie with cream. The cheese and beef fondues served after 4 P.M. are also good Cheap Eats to remember.

TELEPHONE
539 660

METRO
A, Malostranská

OPEN
Daily

CLOSED
Christmas

HOURS
11:30 A.M.–11:30 P.M., continuous service

RESERVATIONS
Suggested during the summer

CREDIT CARDS
AE, MC, V

À LA CARTE
400–600Kč

FIXED-PRICE MENU
Daily 11:30 A.M.–5 P.M., 160Kč, 190Kč, 3 courses, no choices; fondue for two from 4–10 P.M., cheese 400Kč, meat 500Kč

SERVICE
20Kč cover, service included

ENGLISH
Yes, and menu in English

(11) VINÁRNA U MALTÉZSKÝCH RYTÍŘŮ $
Prokopská 10/297, Prague 1

TELEPHONE
536 357, 536 650
METRO
A, Malostranská
OPEN
Daily
CLOSED
Christmas
HOURS
11:30 A.M.–11:30 P.M.;
no food service 3–5 P.M.;
live piano music 7:30–
10:30 P.M.
RESERVATIONS
Advised
CREDIT CARDS
AE, MC
À LA CARTE
500–750Kč
FIXED-PRICE MENU
None
SERVICE
Service included
ENGLISH
Yes, and menu in English

Nad'a Černíková owns and manages one of Prague's most-loved dining choices. Her candlelit Gothic cellar restaurant is in a centuries-old building that once served as a hospice for the Knights of Malta. Every evening, Nad'a rings a chime and tells her guests the stories connected with the building and how she and her husband and two children realized their dream of opening this restaurant.

The menu is short and to the point, listing a few warm and cold appetizers, five or six main courses—which always include fresh fish and a vegetarian plate—three salads, and four desserts, the best of which is Nad'a's own apple strudel served with ice cream and eggnog. Everything is made to order and service can drag out, but sit back and relax in the candlelit cave, listen to the piano player, have a glass or two of Moravian wine, and enjoy Nad'a's tales about the history of this building.

Cafés

(12) CAFÉ SAVOY
Vitězná 5, Prague 1

TELEPHONE
535 000
METRO
A, Malostranská
OPEN
Daily
CLOSED
Never
HOURS
9 A.M.–midnight
RESERVATIONS
Not necessary
CREDIT CARDS
AE, MC, V
À LA CARTE
Snacks and light meals 40–
120Kč
FIXED-PRICE MENU
None
SERVICE
No service charged or expected
ENGLISH
Some, and menu in English

The Café Savoy is a quiet, classic café located at the Malá Strana end of Most Legií (Legion's Bridge) leading over the River Vltava into Staré Město (Old Town). It was established in 1887 and divided into shops in 1915. In 1992 it was restored to its original design with a beautiful hand-painted ceiling. While it is not a place for a full meal, it is a pleasant stop for a light lunch or an afternoon cup of tea and pastry away from the crowds in Old Town.

(13) CHIMÉRA GALERIE-CAFÉ
Lázenská 6, Prague 1

Chiméra is a cozy welcoming café where the devoted regulars settle in for long stays on the old sofas and armchairs or at one of the old tables in the center. The arched room is also a venue for local artists to display their work (and hopefully sell it). There is a mixture of taped jazz and pop music in the background, a limited menu of good toasted sandwiches, wine served by the glass or bottle, and the usual coffee drinks. You will find Chiméra on a pretty little square near Mostecká, the busy street leading to Malá Strana from the Charles Bridge. If you keep on going from the café, you will come to a grassy park that will take you to the burgeoning Kampa section by the bridge.

TELEPHONE
None
METRO
A, Malostranská
OPEN
Daily
CLOSED
Some holidays
HOURS
Noon–11 P.M.
RESERVATIONS
Not necessary
CREDIT CARDS
Not accepted
À LA CARTE
Coffee from 30Kč, toasted sandwiches 34–50Kč
FIXED-PRICE MENU
None
SERVICE
No service charged or expected
ENGLISH
Enough

(14) PETARSTVÍ V KARMELITSKÉ
Karmelitská 20, Prague 1

The locals are here when the doors open, whether to have first crack at the fresh-baked breads or to sit in the café and be served strong coffee and pastries that are as good as they get in this quarter. If you come two or three times, you will be considered a regular by the café staff. If you don't know what to order, look in the bakery display case and point out your selection. The waitstaff are used to this. The poppyseed strudel is good, and so are the heavy seed breads, which are only sold by the loaf.

TELEPHONE
Not available
METRO
A, Malostranská
OPEN
Daily
CLOSED
Some holidays
HOURS
Bakery, Mon–Fri 7 A.M.–7 P.M., Sat 8 A.M.–7 P.M., Sun 10 A.M.–6 P.M.; café, Mon–Fri 8 A.M.–8 P.M., Sat from 9 A.M., Sun from 10 A.M.
RESERVATIONS
Not necessary
CREDIT CARDS
Not accepted
À LA CARTE
Bakery from 15Kč, café 35–100Kč
FIXED-PRICE MENU
None
SERVICE
No service charged or expected
ENGLISH
Limited in bakery, enough in café

Pubs

(15) U KOCOURA
Nerudova 2, Prague 1

TELEPHONE
538 962

METRO
A, Malostranská

OPEN
Daily

CLOSED
Never

HOURS
11:30 A.M.–midnight

RESERVATIONS
Not necessary

CREDIT CARDS
Not accepted

À LA CARTE
60–140Kč

FIXED-PRICE MENU
None

SERVICE
No service charged or expected

ENGLISH
Sometimes

Everyone drinks at U Kocoura (Tomcat), including the help. For years, this smoky beer joint has been a fixture on the corner of the most frequented tourist path to the Prague Castle and St. Vitus Cathedral. Nothing has changed: the haze is still thick, the tables are shared, and the food just an excuse to keep the beer flowing.

STARÉ MĚSTO (OLD TOWN)⸻

Staré Město, or Prague's Old Town, traces its beginnings to 1234. The area revolves around Staroměstské Square and the nearby cobblestoned streets. The square serves as the central meeting point for everyone in Prague, both residents and visitors, as well as a stage for live street theater, with muscans, magicians, mimes, and hawkers—not to mention the crowing costumed man dressed as a rooster—all competing for the best location. The towering bell clock with the twelve apostles appearing on the hour is one of Prague's greatest tourist attractions.

RESTAURANTS

CAFÉS

PUBS

A dollar sign ($) indicates a Big Splurge.

Restaurants

(16) COUNTRY LIFE
Melantřichová 15, Prague 1

TELEPHONE: 2421 3366

METRO: A, Staroměstská

See Country Life in Nové Město, page 48, for a description of this vegetarian restaurant. All other information is the same.

(17) DŮM LAHŮDEK
Malé náměstí 3, Prague 1

TELEPHONE
2423 8024
METRO
A, Staroměstská
OPEN
Daily
CLOSED
Christmas and New Year's
HOURS
Mon–Sat 9:30 A.M.–7 P.M.,
Sun noon–7 P.M.; wine bar,
daily 2 P.M.–midnight
RESERVATIONS
Not necessary
CREDIT CARDS
AE, MC, V
À LA CARTE
Deli sandwiches from 10Kč;
cafeteria, salad bar from 31Kč;
one-plate dinner 60–90Kč;
wine bar 50–240Kč
FIXED-PRICE MENU
None
SERVICE
No service charged or expected
ENGLISH
Yes, and menu in English

Wow, what a place! It looks like Fauchon in Paris, and it has just about as much to offer, with four floors selling gourmet foods and wines from around the world. You name it and chances are excellent you will find it. For prepared food, there's a snack bar, a deli counter with stand-up tables and made-to-order sandwiches, a twelfth-century basement wine bar, and a midlevel cafeteria serving hot dishes throughout the day. The grocery department carries everything you might need to cook your own meals, including Hamburger Helper and peanut butter. In addition, there is a coffee bar, a bakery, meat and fresh fish sections, and a large selection of well-priced wines by the bottle.

(18) KLUB BELLE EPOQUE—ANTIQUE ALMA
Valentinská 7, Prague 1

TELEPHONE
232 5865
METRO
A, Staroměstská
OPEN
Daily in summer, Mon–Fri in winter
CLOSED
In winter, Sat–Sun
HOURS
10 A.M.–6 P.M., continuous service
RESERVATIONS
Not necessary
CREDIT CARDS
AE, DC, MC, V
À LA CARTE
150–350Kč
FIXED-PRICE MENU
None
SERVICE
15Kč cover, service discretionary
ENGLISH
Yes, and menu in English

There is no sign for this restaurant because it is in the basement of a cluttered antiques shop called Antique Alma. The two-level shop is a jumble of dusty collectibles and just plain junk, but it is an interesting place to prowl through and maybe find a treasure or two to take home. The Klub Belle Epoque on the lower level serves as a meeting place for members of the Czech Association of Antique Sellers, but it is also open to the public for light meals served with glasses of good wine. It is an absolutely charming place for a simple lunch of an omelette and a salad, a vegetable plate, or just a glass of nice wine served with caviar and toast. There is also a full-scale restaurant around the corner under the same ownership as the shop, with almost the same menu but a more limited selection of wines.

(19) LOTOS
Platnéřská 13, Prague 1

After a few days in Prague, most Americans will become acutely aware of how fatty and caloric most Czech food is, almost to the point where you can feel your arteries clogging with every bite. A few years ago there would have been no alternative to this path of dietary disaster—other than avoiding a visit to Prague altogether. Fortunately, there are now alternative dining choices for those of us who hope to return home without booking a week at a health farm in order to recover from Czech cooking. One of the best is Lotos, Vera Samkova's natural vegetarian restaurant where the food is prepared without milk or eggs, whole grains are used, seasonings and sweetners are natural, and as much as possible the vegetables are fresh and organic.

Those looking for a light meal will be happy with a bowl of lentil-corn soup, or zucchini soup with smoked tofu, and a trip to the salad bar, where you can dish up small or large portions of oat salad with bamboo shoots and mushrooms, whole-grain pasta with Japanese dressing, or a simple mixed green medley. Main dishes are imaginative in scope, especially the banana ragout with corn polenta, the casserole of Kombu seaweed and vegetables, and the warm broccoli strudel. Desserts are on the boring side, especially the heavy-as-lead ball of millet, raisins, nuts, and coconut. To keep your meal on a healthy track, order a glass of fresh fruit or vegetable juice, an herbal tea, or one of her special drinks of plain almond milk or the one spiked with carrot juice.

TELEPHONE
232 2390

METRO
A, Staroměstská

OPEN
Daily

CLOSED
Christmas

HOURS
11 A.M.–10 P.M., continuous service

RESERVATIONS
Not necessary

CREDIT CARDS
Not accepted

À LA CARTE
100–200Kč

FIXED-PRICE MENU
None

SERVICE
No service charged or expected

ENGLISH
Yes, and menu in English

MISCELLANEOUS
No smoking allowed

(20) METZADA $
Michalská 16, Prague 1

From 1939 until the Velvet Revolution in 1989, there was no full-service Jewish restaurant in Prague. Now there is Metzada (Massada), which I think is one of the most beautiful restaurants in the city. According to Jewish laws, there are separate kitchens and dining areas for dairy (ground level) and meat (upper level). The Chief Rabbi of the Czech Republic has personally inspected the restaurant and has selected the *mashgiachs,* who inspect the premises daily during working hours.

The open, light downstairs is a casual setting with a wonderful collection of old photos of Prague. Here, diners are treated to fish, pastas, and a selection of vegetarian and Jewish specialties. The upstairs is almost

TELEPHONE
2421 3418

METRO
A, Staroměstská

OPEN
Daily

CLOSED
Shabat (unless you reserve ahead, see below)

HOURS
11 A.M.–11 P.M., continuous service

RESERVATIONS
Advised; required for Shabat meals

CREDIT CARDS
AE, MC, V

À LA CARTE
Downstairs (no meat) 200–350Kč, upstairs (meat) 800–975Kč

FIXED-PRICE MENU
Shabat only, lunch or dinner 750Kč

SERVICE
No service charged or expected

ENGLISH
Yes, and menu in English

a museum of what a Jewish home before World War II would have been. All the furniture is authentic from that era, from the comfortable red velvet high-back sofas and the overstuffed chairs that circle the tables to the antique screens that divide them for privacy. The varied menu lists a wide selection of beef and poultry, but the best choices are from the daily menu: perhaps a warm starter of stuffed cabbage rolls or a mixed oriental salad followed by baked or grilled goose breast served with two types of cabbage and potato dumplings. Treat yourself to a bottle of kosher wine and a slice of apple strudel for dessert, and enjoy the romantic ambiance of this very special restaurant in Prague.

NOTE: For Shabat, the restaurant is closed for Friday dinner and Saturday lunch unless you *reserve and pay ahead*. You can do this in person, by telephone, or by email at www.kosher.cz. When you make your booking, request a table upstairs.

(21) U PETRSKÉ VĚŽE $
Petrská 12, Prague 1

TELEPHONE
232 9856

METRO
B, Náměstí Republiky

OPEN
Daily; Sat–Sun dinner only

CLOSED
Never

HOURS
Mon–Fri noon–midnight, Sat–Sun 6 P.M.–midnight, continuous service

RESERVATIONS
Essential

CREDIT CARDS
AE, MC, V

À LA CARTE
600–950Kč

FIXED-PRICE MENU
None

SERVICE
30Kc cover, service included

ENGLISH
Yes, and menu in English

Destination dining at its best—that is the well-deserved reputation Michal Jenik's handsome restaurant maintains with his faithful patrons. Thirty-six places are formally set at tables with white linens over different colored skirts. The attractive glassware was designed after the famed Mosher crystal. Artwork from the well-known Czech artist Kristian Kodet hangs throughout the restaurant. The stained-glass windows depict Prague's most famous landmarks. Be sure to notice the last one, which is not from Prague but from Capri in Italy, where the windows were specially made for the restaurant.

When you are seated, you are served a pot of Czech pork pâté and onions to spread on homemade bread. The menu is an elegant blend of Czech and Continental favorites. In the winter, start with a French onion soup or marinated salmon on buttered toast. Also during the winter, the chef prepares a creditable wild game goulash and grilled medaillons of venison with orange butter and fluffy potato croquettes. House specialties include roast duck served with mushrooms, braised beef in cream sauce, and rabbit on a bed of spinach leaves garnished with grated potato dumplings. Vegetarians are not left out: they can have tagliatelle served three ways, broccoli gratinée, or a spinach and cheese crêpe. A lemon sorbet or warm raspberries ladled over vanilla ice cream are two satisfying ways to end one of the nicest meals you will have in Prague.

(22) UZENINY U RADNICE-MORAVY
Next door to U Radnice 10, Prague 1

The unfriendly place next door is touted for unknowing tourists, who invariably get stuck with a poor meal served by a bored staff with the audacity to smoke on the job. Right nearby is this bustling stand-up eatery patronized by Prague residents who know a good *klobása* when they taste it. The daily menu is written on an easy-to-read plastic menu board. Everything you put in your mouth is sold by weight or priced separately. Want a pickle to go with your big sausage mounded with sauerkraut? Add 7Kč. Mustard or ketchup will set you back an additional 3Kč, bread 2Kč. Those not interested in a fat-laced sausage can order goulash, which is the most expensive dish available and sells for under a dollar. Order a bottle of beer to wash it all down, but don't ask for a glass . . . they don't have them. After you receive your food from the counter, take your plate to one of the stand-up tables and rub elbows with construction laborers, office workers, and other smart Cheap Eaters in Prague. When you are finished, take your dirty dishes to the stand by the industrial scales near the entrance to the kitchen. After this meal, you probably won't want to step on those scales.

TELEPHONE
None

METRO
A, Staroměstská

OPEN
Mon–Fri

CLOSED
Sat–Sun, holidays

HOURS
8:30 A.M.–6 P.M., continuous service

RESERVATIONS
Not accepted

CREDIT CARDS
Not accepted

À LA CARTE
30–45Kč

FIXED-PRICE MENU
None

SERVICE
No service charged or expected

ENGLISH
None, but you won't need it

(23) VINÁRNA V ZÁTIŠÍ $
Betlémské náměstí, Liliová 1, Prague 1

This smart restaurant in Prague's Old Town is very popular and with good reason. The surroundings are pleasing, the quality is dependable, and the food good. There are two sides to Vinárna v Zátiší, the right and the left. For lunch, I reserve a window table on the left side; in the evening, I like the right side, where the black iron furniture with cushioned armchairs and fresh flowers and plants remind me of a winter garden.

The menu beckons with a creative selection of earnest food. To start, you might find cold appetizers of fresh salmon marinated in sea salt and dill and garnished with melon or a gamey venison pâté with cranberry sauce. The grilled tomatoes with mozzarella and basil is a new take on this old favorite. There are always two homemade pastas, one vegetarian. Interesting fish entrées are

TELEPHONE
2422 8977, 2423 1187, 267 848

METRO
B, Národní třída

OPEN
Daily

CLOSED
Never

HOURS
Lunch noon–3 P.M., dinner 5:30–11 P.M., Sun brunch noon–3 P.M.

RESERVATIONS
Definitely advised

CREDIT CARDS
AE, MC, V

À LA CARTE
Appetizers 200Kč, entrées
400–600Kč, desserts 200Kč

FIXED-PRICE MENU
Lunch and dinner, 3 courses
and coffee or tea; price depends
on entrée, from 700Kč for
vegetarian entrée to 1,000Kč
for lamb or venison; Sun
brunch, 110Kč for pancakes,
175Kč for egg dishes

SERVICE
Service discretionary

ENGLISH
Yes, and menu in English

the fish Wellington with salmon and sole and the jumbo
scampi in a walnut and cognac sauce. The Chef's Bohemian Special changes daily and highlights quail and
pheasant in season. The New Zealand lamb chops are
pink and tender, the chicken with rosemary and spring
vegetables light and delicious, and the two vegetarian
main courses better than average. For dessert you could
have another Czech pancake, but why when there is
Amaretto sabayon, chocolate mousse with vanilla sauce,
and warm berries draped over rich vanilla ice cream?

The fixed-price menus for lunch and dinner are priced
according to your choice of a main course and salad, and
they also include any appetizer and any dessert plus
coffee or tea. Wine will be extra. If you do not want such
a big meal, ordering one or two courses is acceptable, but
this is not the place for a little salad and glass of wine for
lunch.

If waffles with maple syrup and fresh fruit, fresh
blueberry muffins, eggs Benedict, eggs Florentine, or
just poached eggs on toast appeal to you, reserve a table
for Sunday brunch.

Cafés

(24) CAFÉ MILENA
Staroměstské náměsti 22, Prague 1

TELEPHONE
2163 2602
METRO
A, Staroměstská
OPEN
Daily
CLOSED
Never
HOURS
10 A.M.–10 P.M.
RESERVATIONS
Not necessary
CREDIT CARDS
None
À LA CARTE
Coffee and pastries from 40Kč,
light meals 40–100Kč
FIXED-PRICE MENU
None
SERVICE
No service charged or expected
ENGLISH
Yes, and menu in English

This coffeehouse is run by the Franz Kafka Society
and is named after Milena Jesenska, one of the famous
author's lovers. The second-floor, 1930s-style room is
simply furnished in black with somber gray walls. It is a
place to remember during the winter, when a seat by the
window gives you a bird's-eye view across the Old Town
square to the astronomical clock with the twelve apostles
appearing on the hour.

The menu consists of soups, sandwiches, and a host of
ice cream creations.

(25) KÁVA KÁVA KÁVA
Národní 37, Nádvoří Platýz (Courtyard Platýz), Prague 1

Coffee specialists Dagmar and Michael Kierans retired to their native home in 1987, after spending twenty-six years in Canada. After awhile, retirement became boring, so they opened this hidden coffeeshop where they sell 100 percent Arabica coffees from around the world to consume here or to take home in bulk.

After you place your order for a latte or cappuccino and a toasted bagel, slice of carrot cake, or banana bread, you will wonder if you really left home. In addition to the coffee drinks and pastries, you can order tea, wine, beer, and soft drinks.

TELEPHONE
Not available

METRO
B, Národní třída

OPEN
Daily

CLOSED
Never

HOURS
Winter, Mon–Fri 7 A.M.–8 P.M., Sat–Sun 9 A.M.–8 P.M.; summer, Mon–Fri 7 A.M.–10 P.M., Sat–Sun 8 A.M.–10 P.M.

RESERVATIONS
Not necessary

CREDIT CARDS
Not accepted

À LA CARTE
Coffee from 60Kč, sweets from 40Kč

FIXED-PRICE MENU
None

SERVICE
No service charged or expected

ENGLISH
Yes, and menu in English

(26) KAVÁRNA OBECNÍ DŮM
Náměstí Republiky 5, Prague 1

After three years of reconstruction, Prague's Municipal House, Obecní Dům, is back in glorious form. This triumph of Czech Art Nouveau is as much of a must-see for visitors as the Charles Bridge. Inside and out, it contains magnificent works of art, including stained-glass windows, appliquéd curtains, and lamps by Alphonse Mucha. Visitors can see the main floor and some rooms in the basement at no charge, but to see the Smetana Hall, Mayor's Rooms, and other areas, you must join a guided tour, which lasts over an hour and is offered three times daily. For more information, call 2200 2100 or 2200 2101.

There are three eating choices in the Obecní Dům: the Kavárna to the left of the main entrance, the Francouzska Restaurace on the opposite side, and the basement wine bar and beer hall. Because the food and the service have yet to match the opulent surroundings, I think for now the best choice is a coffee and pastry or light meal in the Kavárna.

NOTE: Serious Art Nouveau collectors should browse through the Art Decoratif shop, which is just around the corner.

TELEPHONE
2200 2763, 2200 2764

METRO
B, Náměstí Republiky

OPEN
Daily

CLOSED
Never

HOURS
7:30 A.M.–11 P.M.

RESERVATIONS
Not necessary

CREDIT CARDS
AE, MC, V

À LA CARTE
Coffee and pastry from 70Kč, salads 100–130Kč, light meals 100–185Kč

FIXED-PRICE MENU
None

SERVICE
No service charged or expected

ENGLISH
Yes, and menu in English

Pubs

(27) U MEDVÍDKŮ
Na Perštýně 7, Prague 1

TELEPHONE
2422 0930, 2421 1916

METRO
B, Národní třída

OPEN
Daily

CLOSED
Never

HOURS
11 A.M.–11 P.M.

RESERVATIONS
Not necessary

CREDIT CARDS
AE, DC, MC, V

À LA CARTE
50–150Kč

FIXED-PRICE MENU
None

SERVICE
No service charged or expected

ENGLISH
Yes, and menu in English

The "Little Bear" is a restaurant, a pension, and a pub. You want to be in the pub, which is on the right side of the building. If you go to the restaurant, you will pay twice as much, and if you stay in the pension, the noise will keep you counting sheep for hours.

The pub is a big barnlike place where Budvar beer from Česke Budejovice is on tap. The food is a testament to another time and style of cooking, when taste didn't matter much and neither did fat grams nor calorie counts. Go after 3 P.M., order the sausage or liverwurst with vinegary onions as well as a pint of Bud, and leave serious dining for another place.

(28) U ZLATÉHO TYGRA
Husova 17, Prague 1

TELEPHONE
2422 9020

METRO
B, Národní třída

OPEN
Daily

CLOSED
Never

HOURS
3–11 P.M.

RESERVATIONS
Not necessary

CREDIT CARDS
Not accepted

À LA CARTE
30–50Kč

FIXED-PRICE MENU
None

SERVICE
No service charged or expected

ENGLISH
Not much

The red-nosed regulars line up waiting for the doors to swing open at 3 P.M., and soon after, all the well-worn communal tables are filled in one of Prague's most famous pubs, the "Golden Tiger." When President Bill Clinton was in Prague in 1994, he and President Havel lifted a pint or two here, and so has almost every other beer-loving visitor. Food? There are twenty-two choices, ranging from headcheese with onions and vinegar to pork neck served with mustard, pickles, and horseradish. As you can tell, this is not a place to dine; come for a cultural look at what hard-core beer drinking is all about in Prague.

JOSEFOV AND THE JEWISH QUARTER

For centuries, Jews in Prague have inhabited this crowded northern section of Staré Město. Its main street, Pařížská, is a formal tree-lined street leading north from the Old Town square to the Intercontinental Hotel. The Old-New Synagogue is the oldest in Europe. Facing the synagogue is the Ceremonial House, which has a heart-wrenching exhibit of drawings by Jewish children interred at Terezín, the final stop before the Nazi death camps to the east. Also not to be missed is the Old Jewish Cemetery, where due to space problems twenty thousand bodies have been buried ten and twelve deep.

RESTAURANTS

WINE BARS

Restaurants

(29) CHEZ MARCEL
Haštalská 12, Prague 1

Chez Marcel has the look, the feel, and the taste of Paris. A young, good-looking crowd sits around bare wood tables on spindly bistro chairs in two brightly painted yellow rooms. Even the overflowing ashtrays are of French origin.

The menu plays it safe with French favorites such as *charcuterie* (assorted cold meats), *chèvre chaud* (hot goat cheese on lettuce or toast), and a lusty *terrine maison* (house pâté). There is always a *plat* and dessert du jour plus roast chicken with *frites* (fries), beef with four different sauces, pork, rabbit, and two or three vegetarian choices, including quiche. Familiar dessert standbys include *tarte Tatin* (upside-down apple pie), *gâteau au*

TELEPHONE
231 5676
METRO
B, Náměstí Republiky or A, Staroměstská
OPEN
Daily
CLOSED
Never
HOURS
Mon–Fri 8 A.M.–1 A.M., Sat–Sun from 9 A.M., continuous service
RESERVATIONS
Advised
CREDIT CARDS
Not accepted
À LA CARTE
Main-course salads 75–150Kč; 3-course meals 300–475Kč

FIXED-PRICE MENU
None
SERVICE
No service charged or expected
ENGLISH
Yes, and menu in English and
French

chocolat (chocolate cake), and the chef's own crème brûlée. On the weekends from 9 A.M. until noon, omelettes and fried eggs with ham, onions, or mushrooms top the bill of fare.

(30) GOVINDA VEGETARIAN CLUB
Soukenická 27, Prague 1

TELEPHONE
2481 6016
METRO
B, Náměstí Republiky
OPEN
Mon–Sat
CLOSED
Sun
HOURS
11 A.M.–5:30 P.M., continuous
service
RESERVATIONS
Not necessary
CREDIT CARDS
Not accepted
À LA CARTE
Students 40–50Kč, children
and senior citizens 60Kč, others
65–80Kč
FIXED-PRICE MENU
None
SERVICE
No service charged or expected
ENGLISH
Yes
MISCELLANEOUS
No smoking allowed

The Hare Krishna Society seems to have a sect in every city in the world, and Prague is no exception. In the capital city, they operate two vegetarian restaurants, one in the center and one too far in the suburbs for tourists to consider. If you are planning on a meal here, my advice is to arrive when they open and not at the end of their serving time; otherwise your choices will be very limited because when they run out of a dish, that's it.

Servings are huge, and it would be almost impossible for your tab to top 100Kč. Food is dished up cafeteria-style into six-sectioned metal trays that look like those used in prisons. The food is thankfully a quantum leap ahead of its presentation, and it provides diners with hearty, nourishing vegetarian fare that leans heavily toward India for its inspiration. The bread is baked daily and is delicious, as are most of the sweets. Avoid, if possible, the second level, which can get hot and stuffy. Instead, bring your food downstairs where the air is more refined.

NOTE: The second location is at Na hrazi 5, Prague 8; Metro: B, Palmovka.

(31) KAVÁRNA V ANEŽSKÉ
Anežská 12, Prague 1

TELEPHONE
231 0084
METRO
A, Staroměstská
OPEN
Tues–Sun
CLOSED
Mon
HOURS
11 A.M.–9 P.M., continuous
service
RESERVATIONS
Not necessary
CREDIT CARDS
AE, V

If you want to experience Prague before the revolution, come for a meal at Kavárna v Anežské. With no nod to the present and certainly a faint view of the future, the restaurant is a time capsule of Socialist Prague—when orange, dark brown, and beige were the colors of choice, no one considered weight watching to be a concern, and prices were aimed at the proletariat. Today, a meal at Kavárna v Anežské is too cheap for any card-carrying Cheap Eater in Prague to ignore, and with careful ordering, you should be able to finish your dinner without being admitted the next morning for triple bypass surgery.

If you like a cocktail before or after a meal, this is a cheap place to imbibe. A whisky, gin and tonic, or glass of vodka is under $2. During the meal, the wine doesn't come close to $3, and for a *digestif,* a cognac will set you back $2 and an after-dinner liqueur 95¢. A good sign is that the menu doesn't try to cover every culinary base; it merely aims to please the sturdy Czech clientele who keep the place open. Waistline watchers can order the chicken with almond rice or the roast beef; otherwise, most of your selections—whether of beef or pork—will be fried and accessorized with additions of cheese and ham. They do have simple salads, but the vegetables of choice are potatoes and cabbage. *Palačinky* (sweet pancakes) or stewed fruit show up for the finale.

À LA CARTE
140–225Kč

FIXED-PRICE MENU
None

SERVICE
No service charged or expected

ENGLISH
Yes, and menu in English

(32) LE CAFÉ COLONIAL
Široká 6, Prague 1

New on the Prague restaurant scene, Le Café Colonial is a corner café/restaurant that scores big time with trendy Czech yuppies sporting shades and receiving messages on their cellular telephones. The interior has British/French colonial overtones with bright blue, yellow, and burnt orange colors giving it a vibrant and up-market feel.

It doesn't top my list for a serious full-course meal, but I do like it for a morning coffee and croissant, a salad for lunch, or a place to meet someone for a glass of wine in the evening.

TELEPHONE
2481 8322

METRO
A, Staroměstská

OPEN
Daily

CLOSED
Never

HOURS
Bar 8:30 A.M.–1 A.M.; restaurant, lunch 11:30 A.M.–3 P.M., dinner 6:30–11 P.M.

RESERVATIONS
Advised

CREDIT CARDS
AE, MC, V (minimum 1,000Kč)

À LA CARTE
Snacks, light meal 50–150Kč; 3-course meal 250–500Kč

FIXED-PRICE MENU
None

SERVICE
No service charged or expected

ENGLISH
Yes, and menu in English

(33) PIZZERIA RUGANTINO
Dušní 4, Prague 1

Fifty types of pizza plus pasta, salads, sandwiches, and Italian wine tempt Prague Cheap Eaters back on a regular basis. Owner Roberto del Gizzo has a good thing going with his wood-fired, Neapolitan pizzas, which are served here, boxed to take out, or wrapped for delivery anywhere in Prague. You can be plain and simple with a tomato and cheese pizza, go vegetarian with fifteen different possibilities, or go whole hog with the *tonino,*

TELEPHONE
231 8172

METRO
A, Staroměstská

OPEN
Daily

CLOSED
3 days at Christmas

HOURS
Mon–Sat 11 A.M.–11 P.M., Sun 6–11 P.M., continuous service

RESERVATIONS
Not accepted

CREDIT CARDS
Not accepted

À LA CARTE
Pizza 70–160Kč, pasta 130–150Kč, salads and sandwiches 70–120Kč

FIXED-PRICE MENU
None

SERVICE
No service charged or expected

ENGLISH
Yes, and menu in English

MISCELLANEOUS
No-smoking section in front

TELEPHONE
232 0884

METRO
B, Náměstí Republiky

OPEN
Daily

CLOSED
Never

HOURS
Winter 10 A.M.–midnight, summer 8 A.M.–midnight, continuous service

RESERVATIONS
Not necessary

CREDIT CARDS
AE

À LA CARTE
190–250Kč

FIXED-PRICE MENU
None

SERVICE
No service charged or expected

ENGLISH
Yes

loaded with tomato, cheese, ham, mushrooms, artichokes, eggplant, onion, olives, anchovies, and chili peppers. Salads are big, so depending on how many are in your party, agree on one or two and plan to share.

(34) ZLATÁ ULIČKÁ
Masná 8, Prague 1

Nenad Prodanović and his sister, Ljiljiana, run a café with one of the most unusual interiors in Prague. Some call it wierd, others think it's absurd, but I think it's colorful kitsch. From the street it looks like hundreds of others, but the inside is a different story. It has been designed to look like the outside of the quaint cottages on Zlatá Uličká (Gold Street), which is on Castle Hill behind St. Vitus Cathedral and the Prague Castle. To create the inside street setting, the brightly colored little houses along the interior wall have shingles on their roofs and flowers in the windows, and there's a street lamp. You will wonder what the ladder is for until you see the regulars arrive and toss their coats on the rungs.

The decor is different alright—and so is the food. Nenad is Yugoslavian and the food reflects his culinary heritage, which uses spices more liberally than the Czechs do. As usual in a place of this size, pay attention to the daily specials, especially the roast veal, order a side of his creamy mashed potatoes, and let the pizzas go.

Wine Bars

(35) ČESKÁ VINOTÉKA
Anežská 3, Prague 1

A little place with spirit: that sums up Česká Vinotéka, located near the St. Agnes Convent on the fringes of the Jewish Quarter. It opens at 4 P.M., and the two rooms—one with five tables and the other with two tables and four bar stools—fill up rapidly.

Wine drinking is the main event here, not the food. Fifty different types of only Bohemian wines are served, which I was told range from "good to very good." To keep you going with the wine, plates of cheese and meats are served along with small sandwiches.

TELEPHONE
231 1293

METRO
A, Staroměstská

OPEN
Daily

CLOSED
Never

HOURS
4 P.M.–midnight

RESERVATIONS
Not necessary

CREDIT CARDS
Not accepted

À LA CARTE
30–40Kč

FIXED-PRICE MENU
None

SERVICE
No service charged or expected

ENGLISH
Not much, but menu in English

NOVÉ MESTO (NEW TOWN) ———————

Václavské náměstí (Wenceslas Square) and the National Theater are the stellar tourist attractions in this section of town, where the real business of day-to-day Prague takes place. Wenceslas Square is not a square but a wide, tree-lined boulevard—it's where the tanks appeared in the 1968 invasion and where, twenty-one years later, the people declared the Velvet Revolution to be complete. It is now populated by hotels of varying vintages and states of repair, fast-food outlets, and clothing shops, all presided over by strolling crowds by day and pimps and prostitutes by night.

RESTAURANTS

CAFÉS

PUBS

A dollar sign ($) indicates a Big Splurge.

Restaurants

(36) CICALA
Žitná 43, Prague 1

TELEPHONE
2221 0375

METRO
C, I. P. Pavlová

OPEN
Mon–Sat

Buon appetito! For a real taste of Italy in Prague, look no further than Cicala, an Italian family-owned trattoria where the food is as Italian as it gets in this part of the world. Please do not be put off by the dull location and the drab walkway leading to the restaurant's front doors, which are at odds with the inside and the food served. For thirty years Aldo Cicala worked for other people. Now, after saving enough money, he and his family have opened this basement restaurant where they dish up homey Italian soul food and fresh fish dishes.

Typically, there is a tempting antipasti display at the entrance, which is available in small and large portions. The menu has a retinue of pastas with more sauces than you can imagine, but don't look for pizza, as Aldo doesn't serve it. What he does serve with great pride is fresh fish on Tuesday and Wednesday during the winter and Monday through Wednesday in the summer. Since the fish is subject to market availability, I advise you to call and check what's cooking the day you intend to go to avoid disappointment. The creamy tiramisu, prepared by Lucia, Aldo's sweet daughter, is worth the extra hour on the treadmill to work off the calorie onslaught.

CLOSED
Sun

HOURS
11:30 A.M.–10:30 P.M., continuous service

RESERVATIONS
Advised for dinner Fri and Sat

CREDIT CARDS
AE, MC, V

À LA CARTE
300–400Kč without fish; 400–500Kč with fish

FIXED-PRICE MENU
None

SERVICE
No service charged or expected

ENGLISH
Yes, and menu in English and Italian

(37) CORNUCOPIA
Jungmannova 10, Prague 1

Cornucopia is a Prague hot spot where patrons gather to watch big-screen sports on the weekends and CNN on weekday mornings from 7:30 to 9 A.M. The place is small and cramped, with seating along the wall bar and at a few tables in the center of the room. Along the back is the ordering counter where you go to get your food until table service starts around 3 P.M. The one thing you would never expect in a place like this is good food . . . but you will be pleasantly surprised.

Breakfast is served all day from Monday to Friday, and the names of the dishes alone tell you this food is geared to the young and the hungry. Aside from the homemade muffins, the toasted banana bread, or the English muffin topped with an egg, ham, turkey, or tomato and cheese, the Farmer's Breakfast is the lightest: it has three eggs any style, bacon, home fries, and toast. South of the Boarder is a Tums-inducing combination of two scrambled eggs with jalapeño peppers, hot sauce, curried rice, black bean chili, and toast. They are known for their handcrafted sandwiches, which I thought were big enough for two starved teenagers. All the faves are here: egg salad, BLT, ham and cheese, tuna, roast beef, turkey and swiss, club, and brie, basil, and tomato on homemade foccacia bread. Then there is the Rube, which

TELEPHONE
2422 0950, 2423 1992

METRO
B, Národní třída

OPEN
Daily; Sun brunch only

CLOSED
Never

HOURS
Mon–Fri 7:30 A.M.–10 P.M., Sat 9:30 A.M.–8 P.M., Sun brunch 10 A.M.–4 P.M., continuous service; happy hour 4–7 P.M.

RESERVATIONS
Not necessary

CREDIT CARDS
Not accepted

À LA CARTE
Breakfast 75Kč–130Kč, brunch 130–180Kč, sandwiches 75–100Kč, one-dish meals 100–140Kč, salads 50–70Kč, desserts 25–45Kč, drinks 25–40Kč

FIXED-PRICE MENU
None

SERVICE
No service charged or expected

ENGLISH
Yes, and menu in English

is served on a toasted baguette with smoked ham, sauerkraut, melted cheese, and their own secret sauce. The house special, Cajun Chicken, is a fried chicken breast seasoned with spicy bread crumbs and accompanied by lettuce, tomato, and a sour cream and herb dressing.

Not to be forgotten is Sunday brunch, when the place is packed to the rafters with sports nuts watching the game of the moment on the giant-size screen. There are seven choices, ranging from the chocolate and walnut French toast served with fresh fruit to the belt-popping Ranch, with fried chicken, buttermilk biscuits and gravy, three eggs any style, potatoes, beans, and a cinnamon roll. Whenever you have a taste for burritos, black bean chili, or nachos—or yearn for chocolate chip cookies, brownies, or carrot cake—a visit to Cornucopia will fulfill your desires.

(38) COUNTRY LIFE
Jungmannova 1, Prague 1

TELEPHONE
2421 3366

METRO
B, Národní třída

OPEN
Mon–Fri

CLOSED
Sat–Sun

HOURS
Mon–Thur 8:30 A.M.–6:30 P.M., Fri 8:30 A.M.–3 P.M., continuous service

RESERVATIONS
Not accepted

CREDIT CARDS
Not accepted

À LA CARTE
35–125Kč

SERVICE
No service charged or expected

ENGLISH
Some

MISCELLANEOUS
No smoking allowed

The lineup at lunch stretches out the door and down the street. In this calorie-laden city where fat, starch, sugar, and cream are eaten with abandon, it is nice to know that not only is there someplace to eat that is not a guilt trip to a heart attack but that Prague citizens may slowly be realizing that heathy food actually tastes good! The vegetarian food here is prepared by Seventh-Day Adventists, and it is big on tofu, soy, lentils, and homemade bread.

Seating is at tables upstairs, or else you can stand at the window bar, where the people-watching is almost as good as the meal you are eating. There is also a shop in connection with the restaurant selling mostly cereals and a few supplements.

NOTE: There is a second, smaller location in Staré Město. See page 33 for details.

(39) NA RYBÁRNĚ $
Gorazdova 17, Prague 2

TELEPHONE
299 795

METRO
B, Karlovo náměstí

OPEN
Daily; Sun dinner only

When you enter Na Rybárně, you know immediately that all things aquatic are going to be served. The small, two-room restaurant has a colorful aquarium as the main focal point. The first room, with five padded banquettes, also has a seascape mural, while the second room is pleasantly adorned with two antique clocks, white walls, and Oriental rugs on the floors. You don't have to like fish to eat here, but frankly speaking, I wouldn't come here otherwise. And if you love fish, make a point of it, since the restaurant is known for its fresh fish preparations, all priced by the gram.

Fishy appetizers of smoked salmon, crab cocktail, or shrimp soup should get you ready for any of the dozen fish entrées to follow. Trout is cooked in wine, wrapped in cabbage leaves, or barbequed with almond butter. Carp is dusted with caraway seeds, the pike-perch seasoned with chili, and the sea eel dressed with lemon butter. You are on your own for dessert—I have never had room to try the rice pudding, sweet dumplings, or fruit-filled pancakes with ice cream and whipped cream, which always seems too heavy to end of this type of meal.

CLOSED
Never

HOURS
Mon–Sat noon–midnight, Sun 5 P.M.–midnight, continuous service

RESERVATIONS
Advised

CREDIT CARDS
Not accepted

À LA CARTE
3-course meal with fish 590–700Kč, without fish 450–500Kč

FIXED-PRICE MENU
None

SERVICE
10Kč cover, service discretionary

ENGLISH
Yes, and menu in English

(40) OBCHOD ČERSTVÝCH UZENIN
Václavské náměstí 36, Prague 1

In addition to great sausages and beer, Obchod Čerstvých Uzenin has history. It was here that Václav Havel addressed the crowds gathered on Václavské náměstí in the days leading up to the 1989 Velvet Revolution. From its looks today you would never imagine it had any historical significance.

This is a jam-packed, stand-up, Czech-style fast-food joint that serves smoked meats, sausages, and salamis to a beer-drinking crowd. If you like this type of fare, here is a Cheap Eating experience in Prague you should not miss. As with most places like this, you pay first, get your food, and then try to wedge yourself a spot at one of the stand-up tables in the center of the room.

TELEPHONE
None

METRO
A, C, Můstek

OPEN
Daily

CLOSED
Some holidays

HOURS
Mon–Fri 7 A.M.–7 P.M., Sat–Sun 9 A.M.–7 P.M., continuous service

RESERVATIONS
Not accepted

CREDIT CARDS
Not accepted

À LA CARTE
100Kč

FIXED-PRICE MENU
None

SERVICE
No service charged or expected

ENGLISH
None

(41) RESTAURANT ADRIA
Národní 40, Prague 1

Cheap Eaters in Prague should head for the cafeteria section on the mezzanine level of Restaurant Adria. While upstairs is more formal and the service attentive, the food all comes out of the same kitchen, and why pay five times as much for your beef in cream sauce upstairs when you can eat it here for so much less? The cafeteria

TELEPHONE
2449 4621, 2422 8065

METRO
A, C, Můstek

OPEN
Daily

CLOSED
Never

HOURS
10 A.M.–9 P.M., continuous
service in cafeteria
RESERVATIONS
Not necessary
CREDIT CARDS
Not accepted
À LA CARTE
Cafeteria, 50–75Kč
FIXED-PRICE MENU
None
SERVICE
No service charged or expected
ENGLISH
Enough

section is a bright room with modern collages on the walls. Go early for the best selection on the daily changing menu; everything is priced separately, including the bread and butter. If you are not in the mood for a complete hot meal, they offer a range of sandwiches, a salad bar, and the usual gooey desserts.

(42) RESTAURANT MONIKA
Charvátova 11, Prague 1

TELEPHONE
2421 2031, 2421 1622
METRO
B, Národní třída
OPEN
Daily
CLOSED
Never
HOURS
Noon–11 P.M., continuous
service
RESERVATIONS
Advised for the restaurant
CREDIT CARDS
AE, MC, V
À LA CARTE
Deli, 20–50Kč; restaurant,
280–325Kč
FIXED-PRICE MENU
None
SERVICE
No service charged or expected
ENGLISH
Yes, and menu in English

In an area filled with cheap greasy spoons, Monika is a find. Located on a dull back street behind the Tesco department store, it offers two tiers of dining. On the street level is a small deli selling sandwiches and sweets. Remember this if you need a quick coffee and bite to eat after surviving the crowds at Tesco, which also boasts the best supermarket in Prague. For more serious dining at Monika, go downstairs, where there are two sections. The first is light and informal with blond furniture; the second is more intimate and clubby thanks to the dark wood and booth seating. Both have attractive table settings and candles in the evening. The specialties are fish and poultry, and it is possible to order yours grilled, thus avoiding the calorie and cholesterol onslaught that constitutes most meals in Prague. Beef eaters can indulge in any one of five steak variations, ranging from a simple pepper steak to a double thick chateaubriand. The house wine is fine—no need to spend anything more in this department.

(43) ROTISSERIE $
Mikulandská 6, Prague 1

TELEPHONE
2491 2334, 2491 4557
METRO
B, Národní třída
OPEN
Daily; Sun dinner only
CLOSED
Never
HOURS
Lunch Mon–Sat 11:30 A.M.–
3:30 P.M., dinner daily 5:30–
11:30 P.M.

For more than 150 years, the Rotisserie has been one of the best restaurants in Prague for well-prepared Czech food. Nothing has changed. It is formal in the old style with silver candlesticks and shining crystal. The only difference between the fixed-price menus for lunch and dinner is that for dinner you get an appetizer to go with your soup, garnished main course, salad, and dessert. The only drawback with the set menu is that you miss the house specialty—the Bohemian Platter—which includes duck, Prague ham, a chunk of pork, bread dumplings, and red and white cabbage. Pepper steak, also a specialty, appears on both the à la carte and fixed-price menus, as does the goulash. However, if you want the sirloin steak—a beef fillet topped with duck liver pâté—then you'll have to go à la carte. Many main courses are flambéed, as are the desserts, with the possible exception of the banana split.

RESERVATIONS
Advised

CREDIT CARDS
AE, DC, MC, V

À LA CARTE
380–425Kč

FIXED-PRICE MENU
Lunch, 280Kč, 3 courses, no beverage; dinner, 380Kč, 3 courses plus appetizer, no beverage

SERVICE
20Kč cover, service included

ENGLISH
Yes, and menu in English

Cafés

(44) FROMIN
Václavské náměstí 21, Prague 1

The modern, hard edge contemporary design of Fromin makes it look like a place you expect to see in Los Angeles or Las Vegas. The open three-level space atop the Krone building is an architectural sight dominated by a dramatic curved metal stairway leading to the top floor, which pulsates every night with a young disco-dancing crowd.

During warm weather, the wraparound terrace with umbrella-shaded tables is a perfect vantage point for surveying the entire city, including the Prague Castle and St. Vitus Cathedral. Unless you want to join the throbbing disco scene, which hits its stride long after midnight, I suggest going for a morning coffee and pastry or an afternoon ice cream treat whenever you are walking along Václavské náměstí (Wenceslas Square).

TELEPHONE
242 319, 2423 5794

METRO
A, C, Můstek

OPEN
Daily

CLOSED
Never

HOURS
Mon–Fri 9:30 A.M.–2 A.M., Sat–Sun 9:30 A.M.–5 A.M.

RESERVATIONS
Advised after 9 P.M.

CREDIT CARDS
AE, MC, V

À LA CARTE
Light meals 100–200Kč, 3-course meals 375–550Kč, pastries and ice cream 100–150Kč

FIXED-PRICE MENU
None

SERVICE
No service charged or expected

ENGLISH
Yes, and menu in English

(45) GANY'S
Národní 20, Prague 1

No wonder Gany's is perpetually crowded. The location on Národní is central, and the menu goes on forever. You name it and Gany's got it, from a simple bowl of soup to a roast pig (twenty-four-hour notice required). In the morning it is full of coffee drinkers, lunch draws an office crowd, and in the afternoon, ladies in well-worn fur coats and fuzzy hats come for a cup of tea and a few pastries. The menu is too long for everything to be fresh, so concentrate on the chef's specialties—quail, spicy

TELEPHONE
297 655

METRO
B, Národní třída

OPEN
Daily

CLOSED
Never

HOURS
9 A.M.–11 P.M.

RESERVATIONS
Not necessary

CREDIT CARDS
AE, MC, V

À LA CARTE
Coffee and pastry 75Kč, meals 100–300Kč

FIXED-PRICE MENU
None

SERVICE
9Kč cover, service discretionary

ENGLISH
Yes, and menu in English

MISCELLANEOUS
No-smoking room (very boring), half portions for children

chicken wings, and a beef kabob with chili sauce—or something simple like a piece of grilled meat. The access to the restaurant is grim, up two or three flights of dark stairs, which also lead to a pool hall in the back. Forge ahead to the restaurant, where the best seats in the strawberry pink room with cream-colored accents are along the windows overlooking busy Národní třída.

(46) SLAVIA KAVÁRNA
Národní 2, Prague 1

TELEPHONE
Not available

METRO
B, Národní třída

OPEN
Daily

CLOSED
Never

HOURS
8 A.M.–11 P.M.

RESERVATIONS
Not necessary

CREDIT CARDS
AE, MC, V (minimum 500Kč)

À LA CARTE
50–125Kč

FIXED-PRICE MENU
None

SERVICE
8Kč cover, no service charged or expected

ENGLISH
Yes, and menu in English

After some turbulent times and a seven-year closure —when renovation tangled with legal red tape and bureaucratic disputes—Café Slavia reopened in 1997 to rave reviews. Located across from the National Theater, it is still everyone's favorite and within all budgets, from sweet *babičky* totting plastic shopping bags to sleek young things in spray-on black outfits, suave businessmen sealing deals, and politicians plotting their next moves.

The history of the Slavia Kavárna dates back to 1891, when it opened as an imperial café patterned after those in Vienna and Budapest. Over the years it has changed appearances many times—from Art Nouveau to Socialist Realism—but whatever the look, the customers have come and loved it. Writers, artists, revolutionaries, and ordinary citizens have always considered Slavia the café of choice. At one point during the latest restoration project, when problems with American investors rose to a crescendo, its most famous customer, President Václav Havel, warned that relations with the United States could be at stake unless a favorable settlement was agreed upon.

The food consists of hot and cold plates, toasted sandwiches, a few salads, some wonderful pastries, and of course, every coffee drink you could name as well as wine, beer, and mixed drinks.

Bottom line: It's great. Don't miss it.

Pubs

(47) PRVNÍ NOVOMĚSTSKÝ RESTAURAČNÍ PIVOVAR
Vodičkova 20, Prague 1

This popular restaurant and brewery has an underground maze of rooms done in farmhouse decor and accented by a few "painted ladies" on the walls, giving it an appealing character. Diners and drinkers fill the place's 250 seats on a regular basis, spilling out onto the terrace in the summer, and they are served by hardworking waiters in black pants and burgandy aprons who hurry about carrying as many as eight oversized plates at a time. The beer is brewed on the premises, and they prepare some very good food.

The nice thing about the menu is that you can take it easy and order something simple, like a baked potato with garlic and tuna sauce, or go with a group of ten and order a roast suckling pig garnished with potatoes, dumplings, and stewed cabbage (twenty-four-hour notice required). In between are over 150 other choices. House specials include the Brewery Pan (for two to four), which features roast knuckle of pork, chicken, bacon, sausage, potatoes, dumplings, and peas mixed with pearl barley, and the Old Bohemian Platter, a large affair starring pork, smoked meat, grilled sausage, stewed cabbage, potatoes, and bread dumplings. There are eight salads, several soups, five vegetarian dishes, and a good choice of desserts, including apple strudel with nuts and whipped cream.

Not to be overlooked, especially in this brewery, is the beer. The Novoměstský 11 light lager is an unfiltered beer with a 3.2 to 3.4 alcohol content. Because the beer is unfiltered, the yeast remains, making it a source of B vitamins and other minerals. So, order another beer . . . *Na zdraví!*

TELEPHONE
2423 3533, 2423 7552

METRO
A, C, Můstek

OPEN
Daily

CLOSED
Never

HOURS
Mon–Sat 11:30 A.M.–11:30 P.M., Sun noon–10 P.M.

RESERVATIONS
Advised

CREDIT CARDS
AE, MC, V

À LA CARTE
90–300Kč

FIXED-PRICE MENU
None

SERVICE
No service charged or expected

ENGLISH
Yes, and menu in English

(48) U FLEKŮ
Křemencova 11, Prague 1

U Fleků is the most famous pub in Prague. For more than two hundred years, they have been brewing their dark 14 beer and serving it at long black tables to their loyal patrons—who return despite dismal food and surly waiters. Never mind. This is a Prague fixture, and if you

TELEPHONE
2491 5119

METRO
B, Národní třída

OPEN
Daily

CLOSED
Never

HOURS
9 A.M.–11 P.M.

RESERVATIONS
Not necessary
CREDIT CARDS
MC, V
À LA CARTE
90–170Kč, beer 70Kč
FIXED-PRICE MENU
None
SERVICE
No service charged or expected
ENGLISH
Sometimes, depending on your
waiter's mood

like beer, it's also a required stop. Avoid the garden unless you are prepared to pay a surcharge for sitting there.

(49) U KALICHA
Na bojišti 12–14, Prague 2

TELEPHONE
290 701, 291 945, 9618 9600
METRO
C, I. P. Pavlova
OPEN
Daily
CLOSED
Never
HOURS
11 A.M.–11 P.M.
RESERVATIONS
Advised in restaurant
CREDIT CARDS
AE, DC, V
À LA CARTE
180–400Kč
FIXED-PRICE MENU
Lunch, 100Kč, 3 courses, no
beverage
SERVICE
No service charged or expected
ENGLISH
Yes, and menu in English

Touristy? Yes. Corny? Definitely. Then why am I writing about it? Because I think U Kalicha does have something to offer, especially if you go armed with enough information to avoid being ripped off.

According to rumor and legend, Jaroslav Hašek, author of the well-known World War I stories depicting the Czech folk hero Švejk, and Josef Lada, the artist who drew Švejk, drank and ate at this restaurant in Prague. Švejk, the character they created, lives in the heart of every Czech citizen, and Hašek's stories describe a good-natured, perpetually bumbling soldier who's driven mostly by his desire for a good mug of beer and by his belief that friends, delicious food, and laughter can create miracles. Švejk's humor and simple wisdom make the war, the bureaucracy, and the government look ridiculous, and his timeless adventures and philosophy speak to us all.

The restaurant owners, naturally, have capitalized on this sentimental character and provided their guests with an entire wall of shopping possibilities—with the theme of the Good Soldier Švejk prominently displayed on every item. It's up to you if you want to do your T-shirt shopping here or not.

The massive dining room is set up with tables for four to ten patrons, so you can expect to share. In the bar to the left, you can get a bowl of goulash for less than $2 or a lunch menu for under $5. This is the best spot at U Kalicha, where you can't help but notice the autographed pictures of famous people from the worlds of arts and politics who thought so, too. In the dining room, be careful not to fall for the no-price menu, which allows you to eat and drink yourself into oblivion but costs

1,000Kč—or about $30. Live music begins every night around 7:30 P.M., but you have to eat here to enjoy it . . . not just have a beer and linger for hours. The food is basic, and the atmosphere loud. But if you don't mind groups and noise, it can make a somewhat amusing stop.

HRADČANY (PRAGUE CASTLE) ———

The Castle district consists of the imposing St. Vitus Cathedral, which took five hundred years to complete; the Prague Castle itself, which has been the seat of government since the ninth century; the Loreto Church; the Strahov Monastery and its magnificent theological library; and in back of the castle, Zlatá ulička, a row of little buildings where Franz Kafka's sister lived and he often visited.

RESTAURANTS

(50) U Ševce Matouše $ **56**

A dollar sign ($) indicates a Big Splurge.

Restaurants

(50) U ŠEVCE MATOUŠE $
Loretánské náměstí 4

TELEPHONE
2051 4536

METRO
A, Malostranská

OPEN
Daily

CLOSED
Never

HOURS
Lunch 11 A.M.–4 P.M., dinner 6–11 P.M.

RESERVATIONS
Advised

CREDIT CARDS
MC, V

À LA CARTE
300–400Kč

FIXED-PRICE MENU
None

SERVICE
No service charged or expected

ENGLISH
Yes, and menu in English

Carnivore Alert! In Prague, this place is noted for its red meat, and they serve almost thirty versions of steak, from the usual preparations with peppers or onions to one that is definitely destined to raise your fat gram count into heart attack territory, for it is topped with ham and eggs . . . and I suppose cheese if you asked for it. While the food is hardly the quality one would find at a Kansas City steak house, for Prague it is considered to be good. There are some other dishes on the menu, but they are all forgettable, especially anything with fish.

The restaurant is a little hidden; look for the golden boot hanging from under the arcades on the right leading to Prague Castle near Loreta Church. This place has been here forever and nothing has changed. It still has a dark, rather gloomy interior and paper tablemats and napkins. Warning: Watch out for those salted almonds. If you so much as taste one, plan on spending an additional 50Kč—maybe per nut.

OTHER LOCATIONS _____

Vinohrady

This area is home to many crumbling mansions, which serve as testamony to what Prague would have been like without Soviet domination, as well as to the Gothic St. Ludmila Church and the impressive Vinohrady Theater.

RESTAURANTS

CAFÉS

Restaurants

(51) IL RITROVO
Lublaňská 11, Prague 2

It is often the case that some of the best dining choices are a bit off Tourist Central. Il Ritrovo falls into this category. It is about a ten- or fifteen-minute walk from the metro stop I. P. Pavlova. This does not deter the regular Czech clientele, and it shouldn't deter you either, especially if you are yearning for a taste of cucina Italiana. Il Ritrovo is family owned by Beatricea and Antonio Salvatore, and everyone gets into the act, including their daughter, Monica, who helps in the dining room, and Antonio's mother, who taught the chef her recipes for the minestrone, lasagne, gnocchi, and all the pasta sauces, which are made fresh daily.

What to order? Anything that appeals to you: perhaps their special risotto with salmon, caviar, champagne, cognac, cheese, onions, and cream; the simple ravioli with butter and sage; or the *rigatoni della chef*—a rich mixture of mushrooms, cheese, butter, and cream flavored with brandy. For dessert, try their tiramisu or a plate of the Italian cheese. With a good bottle of Italian wine to complement your meal, you won't mind the wait for each course; since everything is made to order, dining here can require some patience.

TELEPHONE
296 529

METRO
C, I. P. Pavlova

OPEN
Mon–Sat

CLOSED
Sun

HOURS
Lunch noon–3 P.M., dinner 6–11:30 P.M.

RESERVATIONS
Advised, especially on weekends

CREDIT CARDS
Not accepted

À LA CARTE
275–350Kč

FIXED-PRICE MENU
None

SERVICE
No service charged or expected

ENGLISH
Yes, and Italian

Cafés

(52) U KNIHOMOLA BOOKSHOP & CAFÉ
Mánesova 79, Prague 2

TELEPHONE
627 7768

METRO
A, Jiřího z Poděbrad

OPEN
Daily

CLOSED
4 days at Christmas and New Year's

HOURS
Mon–Thur 10 A.M.–11 P.M., Fri–Sat 10 A.M.–midnight, Sun 11 A.M.–8 P.M.; live jazz piano Fri and Sat 8–11 P.M.

RESERVATIONS
Not necessary

CREDIT CARDS
AE, MC, V

À LA CARTE
50–150Kč

FIXED-PRICE MENU
None

SERVICE
No service charged or expected

ENGLISH
Yes, and menu in English

U Knihomola, owned by Anne and Alexander Mehdevi, boasts the largest collection of English books available in Prague, with special emphasis on art, literature, travel, reference, and children's books. If you don't find what you are looking for, they will special order it for you and ship it wherever you want.

The basement café is run by an American/Italian husband and wife team, Jason and Elisa Penazzi-Russell. The café, ringed with soft seating, is a comfortable place to sit for an hour or so, have a light meal, and thumb through what you have purchased upstairs. The menu lists daily soups; quiches served with a side salad; carrot, cheese, and chocolate cakes; and Elisa's own tiramisu. For a lazy Sunday lunch, order the Tuscan Picnic, featuring marinated peppers and artichokes, Italian cheese, sun-dried tomatoes, and fresh baked bread. To go with it, sample a glass or two of their featured French, Italian, or Czech wines.

On Friday and Saturday nights from 8 to 11 P.M., there is a jazz pianist (no cover charge), and often during the week, a special book event is planned. The paintings you see are by young artists, and all are for sale.

Smíchov

Mozart once lived in Smíchov, which at that time had a touch of aristocratic class, but today it is a dull factory area. You can visit Bertřamka, the home of František and Josefina Dušek, where Mozart stayed and which is now a museum devoted to these three musicians. You can also visit the famed Barrandov film studios to the south, but beyond that there isn't much to see.

RESTAURANTS

Restaurants

(53) BOTEL ADMIRAL
Hořejší nábřeží, Prague 5 (you'll see the boat!)

During the warm weather, it must be a fight to the finish to snag a waterside table on the terrace-deck of this hotel and restaurant boat docked along the banks of the Vltava River. Even on a snowy day in mid-January, what could be more appealing than sitting inside and looking out over the river to the city beyond? If you are on a budget, plan on this place for a drink at the bar, which is open almost around the clock. The food can run hot and cold, depending on the chef of the moment, and if you aren't careful, tabs can climb. Be wary of the appetizers, which can raise the bill tally in a hurry, and aim instead toward something simple, such as soup and a salad or a grilled pork chop with baked apples. Count the fish out—it is frozen.

TELEPHONE
5732 1302

METRO
B, Anděl

OPEN
Daily

CLOSED
Never

HOURS
Restaurant 11 A.M.–11 P.M., continuous service; bar 7 A.M.–3 A.M.

RESERVATIONS
Advised in the summer for the terrace-deck

CREDIT CARDS
AE, MC, V

À LA CARTE
185–325Kč

FIXED-PRICE MENU
None

SERVICE
Cover 20Kč, service included

ENGLISH
Yes, and menu in English

(54) PRIVAT RESTAURANT AUSTRIA
Štefanikova 25, corner of Kartouzská, Prague 5

Even the name of this restaurant is a reminder of Prague in the days when eating out was something one did only in desperation, and the food is definitely 1970-and-holding. Needless to say, the place needs a bit of spiffing up, starting with the mixed pink, black, and gray wall treatment, the fake flowers, and the passé chair upholstery. But if you are still working on your Ph.D. in fried foods and dumplings, or you are curious about the culinary habits of most Czechs, this is a sure thing. There are separate lunch and dinner menus; the food is basically the same, but after 4 P.M. the prices are higher. If you arrive in the late afternoon, you will be joined by the neighborhood's senior citizens scurrying in to beat the 4 P.M. price hike.

I was amused to read the "low calorie" suggestions. Since when has fried carp with potato salad, roast or fried chicken in butter with potatoes, or chicken fried steak with cheese been on any diet plan? Not on a diet? Then there is the goulash à la Prague served with Czech

TELEPHONE
549 879

METRO
B, Anděl, Štefanikova exit

OPEN
Daily

CLOSED
Never

HOURS
11 A.M.–10 P.M., continuous service

RESERVATIONS
Not necessary

CREDIT CARDS
AE, V

À LA CARTE
125–225Kč

FIXED-PRICE MENU
None

SERVICE
6Kč cover, service included

ENGLISH
Limited

potatoes (that is, fried), potato dumplings, and potato pancakes. Otherwise, there's the Bohemian platter with pork, smoked meat, duck, white and red cabbage, and three kinds of dumplings. Roast duck with cabbage and dumplings would be a safe bet, but off the wall to me are the baked banana rolled in Prague ham and the chicken breast stuffed with salmon and pineapple and cooked in a wine batter. Unless your dish is garnished, plan to pay extra for everything: dumplings and boiled potatoes are 12Kč per serving; butter, an additional 4Kč. Desserts are equally heavy, with pancakes or bananas dressed in chocolate and topped with whipped cream.

(55) U MATOUŠE
Matoušova 6, but entrance at Přeslová 17, Prague 5

TELEPHONE
546 284, 541 877

METRO
B, Anděl

OPEN
Daily

CLOSED
Never

HOURS
11 A.M.–11 P.M., continuous service

RESERVATIONS
Advised

CREDIT CARDS
Not accepted

À LA CARTE
80–120Kč

FIXED-PRICE MENU
None

SERVICE
No service charged or expected

ENGLISH
Some

For a good Czech meal where you will mix with locals, not other visitors, U Matouše is the place to be. The neat and clean dining room has wooden tables set with red placemats trimmed in white. Service is not only honest but friendly and accommodating.

Select a special from the daily menu, or for a rare treat, call seven days ahead and order their special duck, which feeds four to five and costs about 100Kč per person. Otherwise, I like the *domažlická bašta*—smoked pork with potatoes, bread and bacon-flavored dumplings, and red and white cabbage—or *moravský řízek*, a Moravian pork steak served with potato pancakes and cabbage salad. For dessert, the roast apple with cream is a welcome relief. Czech and Moravian wines are poured by the glass or sold by the bottle.

Holešovice

At first glance, Holešovice does not seem like a very inviting place to live, but it does have two green parks and the Gallery of Modern Art.

CAFÉS

Cafés

(56) THE GLOBE BOOKSTORE AND COFFEEHOUSE
Janovského 14, Prague 7

Featuring an inventory of over ten thousand new and used English books, magazines, newspapers, and guide books, the Globe Bookstore and Coffeehouse serves as Prague's home for young literary hopefuls and as a meeting point for expats, and it's a must for visitors eager to be plugged into the current scene.

Sunday brunch draws the lounge lizards, who order poached eggs on olive bread, ham and eggs over easy on a corn muffin, or a plate of scrambled eggs and ham with smoked cheese and served with toast and hash browns. Afterward, they order endless coffees and virtually set up camp at their tables for the rest of the afternoon. There is a set menu during the week: on Monday it's Thai vegetable curry; Tuesday is salmon mousse served with tomato and artichoke salsa and a homemade potato pancake; Wednesday is a ginger-spiked veggie stir fry over rice noodles; Thursday is a spicy peanut chicken crêpe, in which the chicken is sautéed in coconut milk with pineapples and whole dried chilies; and on Friday lap up a tomato or cream pasta served with garlic bread. On the weekend, in addition to brunch, look for Taza Saag, an Indian mix of stewed spinach, chickpeas, and tomatoes served with pita bread. If none of the above specials speak to you, there are salads, sandwiches, homemade soups, yogurt with fresh fruit, smoothies, a full bar, and good brownies.

TELEPHONE
6671 2610

METRO
C, Vltavská, or Tram 5 or 12 and get off at Štrossmayerovo náměstí

OPEN
Daily

CLOSED
Christmas

HOURS
Coffeehouse 10 A.M.–11 P.M., bookstore till midnight

RESERVATIONS
Not necessary

CREDIT CARDS
V (in bookstore only, 350Kč minimum)

À LA CARTE
120–175Kč

FIXED-PRICE MENU
None

SERVICE
No service charged or expected

ENGLISH
Yes, and menu in English

Glossary of Helpful Phrases and Menu Terms

The Czech language is not easy to master, and no one in Prague expects visitors to be fluent. Fortunately, English is now the second language for many people, restaurant personnel generally speak some English. However, it is nice to know a few polite phrases and to be able to look at the menu specials and know what you are ordering.

General Phrases

Do you speak English?	*Mluvíte Anglicky?*
I do not speak Czech	*Ne mluvím Česky*
I do not understand	*Nerozumím*
yes/no	*ano/ne*
hello	*dobrý den*
good evening	*dobrý večer*
good night	*dobrou noc*
goodbye	*na shledanou*
please/you are welcome	*prosím*
thank you	*děkuji*
sir/madam	*pan/paní*
I would like	*chtěl bych*
big/small	*velký/malý*
good/bad	*dobrý/špatný*
open/closed	*otevřeno/zavřeno*

Numbers

0	*nula*
1	*jedna*
2	*dva*
3	*tří*
4	*čtyři*
5	*pět*
6	*šest*
7	*sedm*
8	*osm*
9	*devět*
10	*deset*
11	*jedenáct*
12	*dvanáct*
13	*třináct*
14	*čtrnáct*

15	*patnáct*
16	*šestnáct*
17	*sedmnáct*
18	*osmnáct*
19	*devatenáct*
20	*dvacet*
30	*třicet*
40	*čtyřicet*
50	*padesát*
60	*šedesát*
70	*sedmdesát*
80	*osmdesát*
90	*devadesát*
100	*sto*
1,000	*tisíc*

Days of the Week

Monday	*pondělí*
Tuesday	*úterý*
Wednesday	*středa*
Thursday	*čtvrtek*
Friday	*pátek*
Saturday	*sobota*
Sunday	*neděle*
today	*dnes*
tomorrow	*zítra*
yesterday	*včera*
day before yesterday	*předevčírem*
day after tomorrow	*pozítří*
week	*týden*

Eating Out

Bon appetit!/Cheers!	*Dobrou chut'!/Na zdraví!*
meals	*jídla*
breakfast	*snídaně*
lunch	*oběd*
dinner	*věceře*
menu	*jídelní lístek*
Do you have?	*Máte?*
I am a vegetarian	*Jsem vegetarián/vegetariánka (m/f)*
Please bring the bill	*Prosím dejte mi účet/účet prosím*
Can we pay, please	*Prosím, zaplatíme*
waiter/waitress	*císník/servírka*
fork	*vidličku*
glass	*skleničku*

knife	*nuž*
napkin	*ubrousek*
plate	*talíř*
spoon	*lžíci*

Basic Menu Terms

chléb	bread
cukr	sugar
hořčice	mustard
majonéza	mayonnaise
máslo	butter
ocet	vinegar
olej	oil
omáčka	sauce
pepř	pepper
polévka	soup
sůl	salt
sýr	cheese

Methods of Preparation

dušene	braised/stewed
grilované	grilled
na rošťa, pečený	roasted
smažené	fried
vařené	boiled

Meat (*maso*)

biftek	beefsteak
hovězí	beef
játra	liver
jehněcí	lamb
klobása/párek	sausage
ledvinky	kidneys
šunka	ham
telecí	veal
vepřové	pork

Game (*zvěřina*)

jelení	stag
srnčí	venison
králík	rabbit

Poultry (*drůbež*)

krocan	turkey
kuře	chicken
kachna	duck

husa	goose
bažant	pheasant

Fish (*ryby*)
candát	perch
humr	lobster
kapr	carp
krab	crab
losos	salmon
platýz	plaice
pstruh	trout
sardelka	anchovy
štika	pike
treska	cod
úhoř	eel
velryba	whale
žralok	shark

Salad (*salát*)
fazolový salát	bean salad
hlávkový salát	mixed greens
okurkový salát	cucumber salad
salát z červené řepy	beet salad

Eggs (*vejce*)
míchaná	scrambled
smažená	fried
vařená	boiled
na měkko	soft boiled
se slaninou/šunkou	with bacon/ham

Side Dishes (*přílohy*)
brambory	potatoes
bramborová kaše	mashed potatoes
knedlíky	dumplings
bramborove	potato dumplings
houskové	bread dumplings
švestkové	plum dumplings
krokety	potato croquettes
rýže	rice

Vegetables (*zeleniny*)
česnek	garlic
chřest	asparagus
cibule	onion
čočka	lentils

fazole	beans
houby	mushrooms
kukuřice	corn
květák	cauliflower
okurka	cucumber
mrkev	carrot
rajče	tomato
špenát	spinach
zelí	cabbage

Fruit (*ovoce*)

ananas	pineapple
banán	banana
broskev	peach
citrón	lemon
hrozny	grapes
hruška	pear
jablko	apple
jahoda	strawberry
mandle	almonds
meruňka	apricot
ořechy	nuts
pomeranč	orange
švěstky	plums
třešně	cherries

Dessert (*moučník*)

čokoláda	chocolate
dort	cake
koláč	round, filled pastry
ovocné knedlíky	fruit dumplings
palačinka	crêpes with ice cream and chocolate
šlehačka	whipped cream
žahusek	cake
zmrzlina	ice cream

Drinks (*nápoje*)

čaj	tea
džus	juice
káva	coffee
mléko	milk
pivo	beer
sodovka	soda
víno/bílé, červené	wine/white, red
voda/minerálka	water/mineral water

VIENNA

Vienna's culinary spectrum is as wide ranging as the tastes of its multicultural citizens. The varied cuisine is the result of the meldings of many centuries, in which the many different foods and traditional recipes of the nations of the Austro-Hungarian monarchy were adopted and adapted and given the Austrian touch. The heritage of Austrian dumplings, filled with either meat or fruit, may be found in Bohemia. Viennese *Palatschinken* (thin pancakes with sweet or savory fillings) come via Budapest, and the worthy heir to Italian veal piccata Milanese is the ever-popular *Wiener Schnitzel.*

Dining in Vienna runs from a *Würstelstand* on the street corner dispensing cheap and juicy sausages on thick rolls to world-famous restaurants serving luxurious gourmet cuisine. Cheap Eaters will find good values in *Beisl*—Viennese neighborhood bistros. These small restaurants, found on almost every block, serve traditional Viennese cooking at prices to fit all budgets. Many *Beisl* put chairs and tables out on the pavement during the summer months to serve guests in improvised gardens, called *Schanigarten.*

Cheap Eats in Vienna is divided into sections by establishment type. First, restaurants are listed according to area, followed by coffeehouses, tearooms, pastry shops, and finally *Heurigen*—wine taverns in the Vienna Woods. Wherever you may decide to go . . . I wish you *Guten Appetit!*

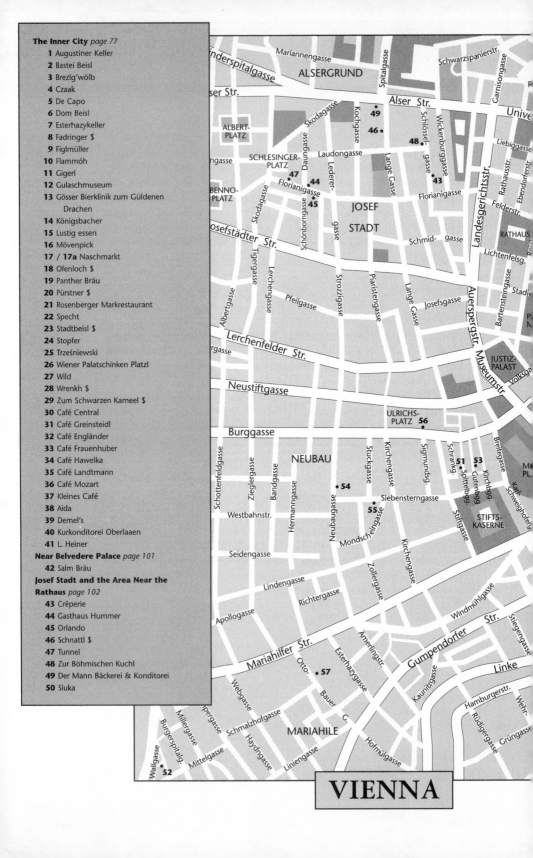

VIENNA

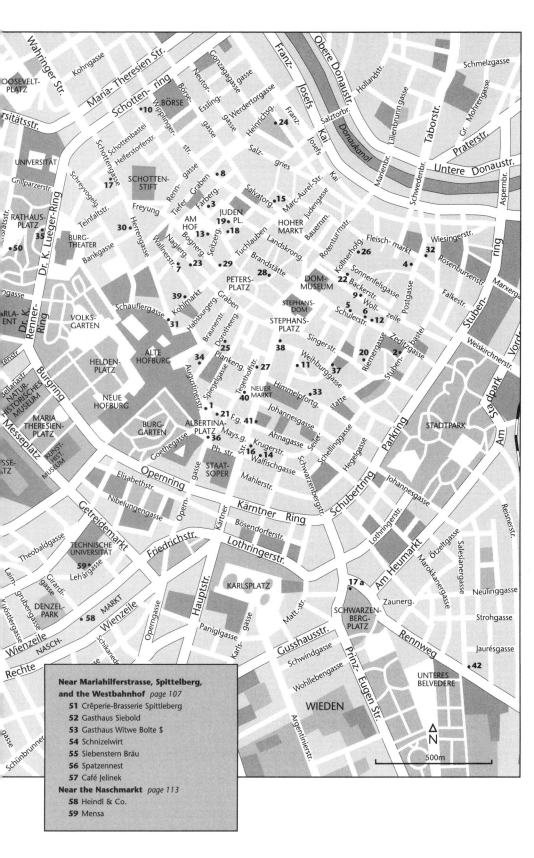

Cheap Eating Tips in Vienna

1. The first two commandments for Cheap Eating in Vienna are, one, check the menu posted outside to see if it is within your budget and offers something you want to eat and, two, stick with the chef's daily specials.

2. The Cheapest Eat will be the fixed-price lunch (*Tagesmenü*), which is either a one-dish garnished plate or a two-course meal.

3. When you are handed the regular English menu, always ask to see the daily specials menu as well—even though it is usually only in German, it always represents the best efforts of the chef.

4. Bread is usually extra. You will pay by the pieces you consume, not by the basket of bread served. If you don't eat the bread, be sure to remind the waiter, since you are not required to pay for it to sit on your table untouched.

5. To the delight and convenience of many Cheap Eaters in Vienna, most restaurants stay open all day long and serve full meals continuously. But remember, lunch specials end around 2 P.M., or even earlier if they run out.

6. In a coffeehouse, the price of coffee may seem expensive, but it buys you the right to occupy the table indefinitely.

7. If you eat a meal in a coffeehouse, do it at lunch when many offer special Cheap Eating menus. Ordering à la carte in a café is a sure way to have an expensive meal.

8. Forget ordering bottled water and vintage wines. The local water is perfectly safe, and the house wines are usually very pleasant.

9. Picnics are a wonderful way to stretch your Cheap Eating budget, and the corner bakery is the best place to shop for them. Here you can select from a case full of freshly cut sandwiches, pick up a pastry or two, and usually buy a bottle of water or a soft drink from a cooler in the corner.

10. Another Cheap Eat is to have a fat *Wurst* wrapped in a fresh roll at the corner *Würstelstand.* These sausage treats come in all sizes and tastes, and they are not only quick and delicious but within any budget.

11. A majority of restaurants display the sign *Sonntag Ruhetag,* which means closed on Sunday. Also watch out for summer and other vacation closings, many of which vary from published dates, or else they are not decided upon or announced until a few days

before the restaurant actually closes. To avoid disappointment, call ahead to check.

12. The tip (10 to 15 percent) is usually included in the final bill as a service charge, or else it is not expected at all. However, rounding off the total is always appreciated.

13. Crimes and misdemeanors by waiters tallying your restaurant tab are rare in Vienna, but they do happen. Always check your bill carefully, and question anything you do not understand.

General Information about Cheap Eating in Vienna

Vienna combines the splendor of a capital city with the familiarity of a village.
—*Patrick Leigh Fermor,* A Time of Gifts, *1997*

Where to Eat

Start your day with a coffee and pastry in a *Konditorei* (bakery), a café, or a bar. For lunch, look for daily specials offered in many cafés or sample a juicy *Wurst*, either boiled or grilled, at a corner *Würstelstand*. For both lunch and dinner, choices range from formal restaurants to *Beisl* (Austria's version of the French neighborhood bistro) and *Gasthäuser* (informal, simple restaurants). In the afternoon, cakes and coffee are taken in a *Kaffeehaus,* or more informally, in a *Konditorei* that has stand-up bars or tables. Not to be overlooked are the *Heurigen*—wine taverns located on the outskirts of Vienna that open late in the afternoon and provide buffet meals to accompany their wines—and *Bierstube,* beer parlors similar to English pubs, which serve beer and food.

What to Eat

The Viennese love to eat, and they often do so up to five times a day. They start with a light Continental breakfast of fresh rolls and strong coffee, then around 9 A.M. they have what is called *Gabelfrühstück*—a fork breakfast with eggs, cold meats, sausage, or maybe a bowl of goulash. Lunch, served between noon and 2 P.M. is hearty, and for many it's the main meal of the day. *Jause,* afternoon coffee and cake, is the teatime meal, and finally, dinner (often a light meal, and no wonder) is served between 6 and 9 P.M.

In Vienna, cholesterol-rich, high-calorie foods still make up most of the daily diet. However, with some careful planning, you *can* eat healthy when visiting Vienna. The sinfully rich dishes are still there, but the discerning Cheap Eater can choose, for instance, whether to have succulent pork roast with dumplings and gravy or the less fattening *Tafelspitz* (the favorite meal of Emperor Franz Joseph I), which is boiled beef tenderloin served with apple-flavored horseradish, chive sauce, and roast potatoes. For a light starter, sample a bowl of *Frittatensuppe,* consommé with thinly cut pancake slices floating on top. Everyone wants to have *Wiener Schnitzel,* but for the real thing, make sure yours is made with veal, not pork.

And finally, there are Viennese pastries, which constitute a wonderous world of unlimited sweet decisions.

Viennese Pastries

Never trust a culture that doesn't value chocolate.

—Anonymous

There is an unwritten law in Vienna that all visitors must suspend calorie worries and dietary constraints for the duration of their stay. To list all the pastry temptations you will encounter would take another volume. At Demel's there are over sixty choices of pastry alone, not counting the ice cream and confections, and at all of the best pastry shops—who of course do all of their own baking—you can view the entire panorama layered in glass display cases. Try not to think of these divine pastries as a guilt-ridden indulgence. Instead, consider them culinary research. Do you prefer *Kaiserschmarrn*—Emperor's trifle, another of Emperor Franz Joseph's favorites and named after him— or *Topfenknödel, Guglhupf,* or *Mohnstrudel?* You will, of course, try *Sachertorte* . . . at both Demel's and at the Sacher Hotel. Why both? Because that is the only way you will be able to judge which is best.

Here is a short list of a few of the most popular choices.

Apfelstrudel	Apples, raisins, and cinnamon wrapped in a pastry dough and baked until golden; often topped with whipped cream
Dobostorte	A Hungarian cake made with layers of sponge cake and chocolate icing
Guglhupf	Plain or marble cake
Linzertorte	Jam tart made with almond pastry
Mohnstrudel	A heavy dough with poppyseeds inside; sometimes raisins are added
Sachertorte	Basically a chocolate cake with apricot jam and chocolate icing
Topfenstrudel	Sweet cheese, instead of apple, fills the strudel

What to Drink

Drink the local wines served by the glass or pitcher in all but the fanciest addresses; the dry, fruity white wines are the most popular. The best place to try Austrian wines is in one of the *Heurigen* on the outskirts of town (see page 115). As for the beer, it is just as popular as the wine, and the light or dark Grosser Brau from Styria is a full-bodied choice. An hour or two spent in a Viennese coffeehouse is a must. These Vienna institutions have long-standing traditions and are considered important daily meeting places for people from all walks of life.

Viennese Coffeehouses

There are fewer psychiatrists per capita in Vienna than in any other major Western city. That is because of the coffeehouses. At these places you talk about your problems for hours with complete strangers. You never intend to see them again, so you say anything.
—*Peter Weiser, director of the Mozart bicentennial in Vienna*

After the Turkish siege of Vienna in the sixteenth century, the city's first coffeehouse was opened by G. Kolschitzky, a Turkish interpreter who was given that mandate along with five hundred sacks of coffee. He adapted the strong Turkish brew by adding milk, thus the popular *Melange* was born. In 1700, Emperor Leopold I granted the license to sell coffee to four other persons, and by the middle of the eighteenth century, everything you find in a Viennese coffeehouse today was in place: newspapers, card games, billiards, and the glass of water served on the tray with the coffee. The coffeehouse has always been a meeting place for personalities in politics, business, art, and culture, and many decisions affecting Austria's fate have been made in them. Some have become legends in their own right; others may be lesser known but are just as appealing.

In the coffeehouse, everyone is equal—rich, poor, young, or old. To the Viennese, the daily trip to their favorite coffeehouse is an integral ritual, where they read, have a chat, and perhaps write, sketch, or compose works that, who knows, may someday change the direction of history. For the price of one small coffee, you can sit all day undisturbed—no one will ask you to leave. Today, many coffeehouses have expanded meal operations and serve a hot lunch, usually a traditional Viennese meal of a hot soup and a main course. These are usually good Cheap Eat buys, but if you order à la carte, be very careful because the meal can rapidly add up to anything but a Cheap Eat in Vienna.

Coffee is not just coffee in Vienna. The following is a primer in Viennese coffee to help get you started. When ordering coffee, you need to first decide if your coffee will be small (*kleiner*) or large (*grosser*). Whatever your order, the waiter will bring it to you on a silver tray with a glass of water and a spoon.

Brauner	Black coffee with a little milk
Einspanner	Mocha in a glass with whipped cream
Kaffee mit Schalagober	Most traditional coffee, topped with whipped cream or *Doppelschlag* (double whipped cream)
Maria Theresia	Black coffee with orange liqueur added
Mokka	Black coffee flavored with mocha
Melange	Coffee with equal amounts of frothed milk and coffee, sometimes topped with whipped cream

Pharisäer	Coffee in a glass, with whipped cream and a glass of rum on the side
Schwarzer	Black coffee with nothing added
Türkischer	Turkish coffee; about as strong as coffee gets—brewed with grains and sugar in a copper pot
Wiener Eiskaffee	Strong, cold mocha with vanilla ice cream and whipped cream

Reservations

As in any major European city, the better the restaurant, the more essential it is to reserve a table. In any Big Splurge restaurant advance reservations are almost required, and just to be on the safe side, even if I only suggest making reservations, go ahead and make them for all but the most modest establishments.

Paying the Bill and Tipping

In Vienna, bill padding is not an accepted practice, as it is in Prague, and mistakes in the tally are few. However, this is not to say that errors never happen because they do. Wherever you are eating, always check the figures on your bill carefully and question any charges you do not understand. All of the *Cheap Eats* listings state whether or not the service charge is included, and if not, whether a tip is expected (discretionary) or not expected. Many restaurants include a 10 to 15 percent service charge. Even so, it is customary to round off the bill or add 5 percent extra, depending on the type of restaurant and the service you received. If there is no service charge but a tip is expected, leave 10 to 15 percent. If a tip is not necessary, you are off the hook unless you want to round off the total.

Holidays

Shops, museums, banks, and many restaurants are closed on the following days.

January 1	New Year's Day
January 6	Epiphany
March/April, dates vary	Easter
	Easter Monday
May 1	Labor Day
6th Thursday after Easter	Ascension Day
6th Monday after Easter	Whit Monday
Mid-May, dates vary	Pentecost Sunday and Monday
End of May, date varies	Corpus Christi
August 15	Assumption Day
October 26	National Day
November 1	All Saints' Day
December 8	Immaculate Conception
December 25–26	Christmas

Finding an Address

Finding your way around Vienna is not particularly difficult, but note that all Viennese addresses begin with a district code, which appears as either a four-digit code, a roman numeral, or a regular arabic numeral. All the addresses in *Cheap Eats in Vienna* use the four-digit code, which is preceded by the letter A. The middle two numbers of the code tell you the district; you don't need to worry about the first or fourth numbers. Following the code is the street name and the street number. For example, an address in the first district would read "A-1010, Singerstrasse 14." An address in the eighth district would read "A-1080, Florianigasse 3." However, elsewhere in Vienna, you may see the same address as "8, Florianigasse 3," or "VIII, Florianigasse 3."

Transportation

Taxi drivers are honest and the Vienna transportation system is safe and easy to use. All *Cheap Eats* listings give the nearest U-Bahn (subway) stop as well as the line numbers you can take to get there. If you are going to be in Vienna for a few days, look into the Vienna Card, which entitles you to unlimited travel on the subway, buses, and trams as well as discounts at some museums, restaurants, and shops. The Vienna Card is available at tourist information offices, public transport centers, and in some hotels.

Restaurants in Vienna by Area

INSIDE THE INNER RING (THE INNER CITY)

The Innere Stadt (Inner City), which has been the heart of the city for two thousand years, is characterized by its most striking landmark, the magnificent Gothic cathedral Stephansdom (St. Stephen's Cathedral). Concentrated here are many of the city's major museums, churches, the Hofburg (which houses the Spanish Riding School), the state opera, hotels, restaurants, and fine shopping along the Kärntner Strasse, Graben, Kohlmarkt, and Herengasse.

RESTAURANTS

(1)	Augustiner Keller	**78**
(2)	Bastei Beisl	**79**
(3)	Brezlg'wölb	**79**
(4)	Czaak	**80**
(5)	Da Capo	**81**
(6)	Dom Beisl	**81**
(7)	Esterhazykeller	**82**
(8)	Fadringer $	**82**
(9)	Figlmüller	**83**
(10)	Flammóh	**83**
(11)	Gigerl	**84**
(12)	Gulaschmuseum	**84**
(13)	Gösser Bierklinik zum Güldenen Drachen	**85**
(14)	Königsbacher	**86**
(15)	Lustig essen	**86**
(16)	Mövenpick	**87**
(17)	Naschmarkt, Schottengasse	**87**
(17a)	Naschmarkt, Schwartzenbergplatz	**87**
(18)	Ofenloch $	**88**
(19)	Panther Bräu	**88**
(20)	Pürstner $	**89**
(21)	Rosenberger Marktrestaurant	**89**
(22)	Specht	**90**
(23)	Stadtbeisl $	**90**

A dollar sign ($) indicates a Big Splurge.

Restaurants

(1) AUGUSTINER KELLER
Der Stadtheurige bei der Oper
A-1010, Augustinerstrasse 1

TELEPHONE
533 10 26, 533 09 46

U-BAHN
1, 2, 4, Karlsplatz

OPEN
Daily

CLOSED
Never

HOURS
11 A.M.–midnight, continuous service; dinner buffet Tues and Thur from 6:00 P.M.

RESERVATIONS
Not necessary

CREDIT CARDS
AE, MC, V

À LA CARTE
200–240AS

Well-positioned just off the Kärntner Strasse and behind the Opera is Augustiner Keller, a large underground restaurant with brick arches, wooden tables covered with red-and-white cloths, and hard black Tyrolean chairs. The waitstaff is red-cheeked and jolly, and so are most of the diners. The Tuesday and Thursday dinner buffet draws the crowds, and live music every night from 6:30 P.M. insures a tourist presence.

The menu covers all the bases, from pork schnitzel and grilled or fried chicken to steak smothered in onions, all garnished with dumplings, potatoes, or sauerkraut. Lighter appetites will appreciate the cold meat and cheese plates, or the large mixed salad. Desserts? More dumplings, this time filled with fruit; ice cream slathered in chocolate sauce and whipped cream; and of course, cheese or apple strudel.

(2) BASTEI BEISL
A-1010, Stubenbastei 10

The Bastei Beisl is a plain-Jane spot about five minutes east of Stephansplatz. The uncluttered interior has dark wood booths and benches on one side and a rather formal dining room on the other, set with linens and offering diners comfortable chairs as opposed to benches. The Cheap Eats here are either of the two fixed-price lunch menus, which change daily but offer neither a choice nor a beverage. If you like fried food, you will love the cook's renditions of pork and veal schnitzels, the cordon bleu, or the grilled beef cutlet covered with fried potatoes and onions. The fish is all frozen, so it can be avoided. For the grand finale (if you don't mind more fried food), try the sizzled apples and cranberries sprinkled with sugar.

(3) BREZLG'WÖLB
A-1010, Ledererhof 9

Arm yourself with a detailed map and plan to get lost in the search for this historic and romantic restaurant. The street, Ledererhof, is sandwiched tightly between Färbergasse and Judenplatz, not too far from the Kirche am Hof. The restaurant has a colorful past as a bakery and a tannery, and this history is on display everywhere you look. The inside is dark, both upstairs and in the cellar, where candles burn both day and night, giving it an intimate feel. In the summer, you may want to forgo the romantic candlelight for a table on the sunny terrace.

The menu stresses old Viennese cooking and goes on forever. When ordering, be careful because everything is

FIXED-PRICE MENU
Tues and Thur dinner buffet, 195AS, includes wine and dessert

SERVICE
Service included

ENGLISH
Yes, and menu in English

TELEPHONE
512 43 19

U-BAHN
1, 3, Stephansplatz or 3, Stubentor

OPEN
Mon–Sat

CLOSED
Sun, holidays

HOURS
Mon–Fri 9 A.M.–midnight, Sat 11 A.M.–3 P.M., 6 P.M.–midnight

RESERVATIONS
For dinner

CREDIT CARDS
AE, DC, MC, V

À LA CARTE
150–220AS

FIXED-PRICE MENU
Lunch (noon–3 P.M.), 90AS, 2 courses, and 110AS, 3 courses, no beverage

SERVICE
25AS cover in the evening, service included

ENGLISH
Yes, and menu in English

TELEPHONE
533 88 11

U-BAHN
1, 3, Stephansplatz

OPEN
Daily

CLOSED
Never

HOURS
11:30 A.M.–1 A.M., continuous service

RESERVATIONS
Suggested for dinner or for the summer terrace

CREDIT CARDS
AE, DC, MC, V

À LA CARTE
185–250AS

FIXED-PRICE MENU
None

SERVICE
Service included

ENGLISH
Yes, but no menu in English

priced separately, even the pats of butter. Cheap Eaters will be wise to set their sights on whole-meal dishes such as the *Tafelspitz,* the famous Viennese boiled beef garnished with potatoes; roast pork served with sauerkraut and dumplings; or the beef goulash, with its obligatory potatoes and dumplings. For lunch, the spinach strudel with a light garlic sauce or one of the large salads featuring cold pork or tuna will get you by. Dessert lovers will not want to miss the chef's sweet cheese strudel covered in vanilla sauce.

NOTE: The area is filled with interesting boutiques that are well worth a few minutes of window shopping. While in the neighborhood, please don't miss the beguiling Teddy Bear Museum and shop, just around the corner from the restaurant at Drahtgasse, 3.

(4) CZAAK
A-1010, Postgasse 15

TELEPHONE
513 72 15

U-BAHN
1, 4, Schwedenplatz

OPEN
Mon–Sat

CLOSED
Sun, holidays

HOURS
Mon–Fri light snacks
8:30 A.M.–11:30 A.M.,
full menu 11:30 A.M.–
midnight, Sat 11 A.M.–
midnight, continuous service

RESERVATIONS
Suggested

CREDIT CARDS
Not accepted

À LA CARTE
120–175AS

SERVICE
Service discretionary

ENGLISH
Yes

Werner Czaak and his son, Peter, are carrying on the family tradition of running this restaurant, which was founded in 1928 by Werner's grandfather. Today it is still going strong, and in my book, a real winner in Vienna. Not that it is anything flashy or fancy—it is neither. Near the entrance, the bar is home to a number of regulars who swap war stories and act as unofficial hosts to any newcomer. Unless you want to banter through the meal with these bar fixtures, keep on going toward the back and sit at the tables, which have been continually filled with contented diners ever since the place opened sixty-plus years ago.

There is a weekly changing menu of à la carte items, plus a coterie of Vienna standbys. The schnitzels are garnished with a salad, and the beef minute steak is served with braised onions and potatoes. For lunch, I love the goulash soup with a piece or two of hearty bread to mop up the last drop, or if I am feeling virtuous, perhaps the chef's salad. For dessert, I always hope to see the bread pudding, made from rich brioche covered in bright red raspberry syrup. The servings are generous, there is no cover charge, and Werner and Peter Czaak are warm and gentle hosts who will make you feel welcome whenever you are lucky enough to be in Vienna.

(5) DA CAPO
A-1010, Schulerstrasse 18

For a welcome change of pace, come to this authentic Italian *ristorante* for an afternoon or evening of good Italian food and hospitality. There is no pretense here: you sit at bare tables in the brick cellar or on the summer terrace, and you choose from two menus—a short seasonal one, which changes every few weeks and highlights the best the market has to offer, and the regular menu. I always pay attention to the seasonal menu, which features fresh fish. In the late fall, I look for the spaghetti with scampi or the rich chicken livers, which are served with parsleyed potatoes. The extensive regular menu has something to appeal to everyone. Its seven or eight salads can be meals in themselves. There are also twenty-three varieties of wood-fired pizza, seven classic pastas (including a sampler plate of three), chicken roasted with rosemary and served with rice, veal Marsala or piccata, and fillet steak garnished with grilled tomatoes and herbed potatoes.

If chocolate is your passion, hope that the diet-defying *Torta di Cioccolata "Da Capo,"* a decadent slice of chocolate cake served with warm chocolate sauce, is on the menu. Otherwise, there is always tiramisu or, for a light finish, lemon sorbet splashed with prosecco.

TELEPHONE
512 44 91

U-BAHN
1, 3, Stephansplatz

OPEN
Daily

CLOSED
Never

HOURS
11:30 A.M.–midnight, continuous service

RESERVATIONS
Suggested, especially for summer terrace

CREDIT CARDS
Not accepted

À LA CARTE
200–270AS

FIXED-PRICE MENU
None

SERVICE
Service included

ENGLISH
Yes, and menu in English and Italian

(6) DOM BEISL
A-1010, Schulerstrasse 4

This neighborhood *Beisl* is packed to the walls at lunchtime with a weekday crowd of robust regulars who show up for the sturdy daily specials. No one speaks English, and no one cares whether you speak German. The tables are either bare or dressed with red oilcloths, and the smoky atmosphere is lively and authentic. The one long-suffering waitress, who also doubles as the cashier, can serve six mugs of beer while memorizing the orders from all the tables and somehow get it all right. The chef in the open kitchen never misses a beat, and the owner tends bar.

The daily specials are what to order, and because they are so filling, this will not be the place to think about dessert.

TELEPHONE
512 91 81

U-BAHN
1, 3, Stephansplatz

OPEN
Mon–Thur; Fri lunch only

CLOSED
Sat–Sun, holidays

HOURS
Mon–Thur 11 A.M.–7 P.M., Fri 11 A.M.–3 P.M.

RESERVATIONS
Not necessary

CREDIT CARDS
Not accepted

À LA CARTE
80–130AS

FIXED-PRICE MENU
None

SERVICE
Service included

ENGLISH
None

(7) ESTERHAZYKELLER
A-1010, Haarhof 1

TELEPHONE
533 93 40
U-BAHN
3, Herrengasse
OPEN
Daily
CLOSED
Never
HOURS
Mon–Fri 11 A.M.–11 P.M., Sat–
Sun 4–11 P.M., continuous
service
RESERVATIONS
Not necessary
CREDIT CARDS
Not accepted
À LA CARTE
100–150AS
FIXED-PRICE MENU
None
SERVICE
Service included
ENGLISH
Yes

As you enter from the street, make your way down a long flight of stairs to this casual wine cellar, which has been a fixture on the Vienna eating and drinking scene since 1683. At a wine cellar, the emphasis is on drinking, and the food is designed to be filling rather than gourmet.

Here it is all buffet, and each item is sold separately. You don't need to speak German to select what you want from behind the glass case, then you take your food to a table, where you will be served your wine by a waitress. The food choices include salads, cheeses, sausages, bread, and one or two warm dishes, which might be microwaved.

(8) FADRINGER $
A-1010, Wipplingerstrasse 29

TELEPHONE
533 43 41
U-BAHN
1, 3, Stephansplatz
OPEN
Mon–Fri
CLOSED
Sat–Sun, holidays
HOURS
Lunch 11:30 A.M.–3 P.M.;
dinner 5:30–10 P.M.
RESERVATIONS
Essential
CREDIT CARDS
None
À LA CARTE
Lunch or dinner 375–450AS
FIXED-PRICE MENU
Lunch only, 150AS, 3 courses;
lunch or dinner, 390AS,
3 courses, includes cover and
service
SERVICE
25AS cover, service
discretionary
ENGLISH
Yes

For a quiet meal in beautifully stylish surroundings, book a table at Fadringer, recognized as one of the best restaurants in Vienna. True, it is very easy to go all out here and find yourself in the middle of a Big Splurge. But if you go for lunch and take advantage of the bargain three-course daily menu, you will have one of the most delicious Cheap Eats around.

The restaurant displays changing art exibits in two rooms with rather closely placed tables, each with its own bouquet of flowers and pink linens with white overlays. In the first, the Oriental rug on the floor adds warmth and a touch of formality. The back room has banquettes with hard seats and padded backs. Waiters wear bow ties and vests and provide pleasant service.

The chef prepares somewhat lighter adaptations of Viennese cuisine. The bargain set-lunch menu changes daily and keeps the business crowd coming back for more. You might start your meal with a leafy green salad or an herb cream soup flavored with bits of ham. There is no choice for the main course, which is either a meat or a fish dish liberally garnished with vegetables, potatoes, or a side salad. Desserts offer no choice, but who cares when you can have a vanilla strudel with fresh raspberry sauce.

If you decide to go à la carte or have the more expensive fixed-price menu, you will have a very nice and well-worth-it Big Splurge meal. On a cold night, I like to start with the gnocchi with spinach and cheese, or maybe the soup of the day, followed by veal with truffle sauce, garnished with asparagus and butter noodles. For dessert, I can't resist the chocolate chestnut mousse surrounded by dates, grapes, and figs.

(9) FIGLMÜLLER
A-1010, Wollzeile 5

Figlmüller is a great place that everyone loves. Open daily and serving continuously, it packs in tourists and locals alike, who don't mind sitting comfortably close to one another in several little rooms, all illuminated by wrought-iron lights. The restaurant is located in a small boutique-lined passage between Wollzeile and Backerstrasse. If you arrive during peak times, or for Sunday lunch, plan on a wait, though this will give you time to browse along the walkway. While you probably won't be interested in the shop selling electric lights, or the one featuring four-inch stiletto-heel shoes, the antique shop and the store displaying Austrian clothing are appealing.

When seated, don't worry about trying to decipher the menu, which is scribbled on a green chalkboard. When you come to Figlmüller, order only their famous specialty: *Wiener Schnitzel* and a green salad, washed down with a pitcher of wine from the owner's vineyard. Beer, coffee, dessert? Not here, because they are not served.

TELEPHONE
512 61 77

U-BAHN
1, 3, Stephansplatz, or 3, Stubentor

OPEN
Daily

CLOSED
Aug

HOURS
11 A.M.–10:30 P.M., continuous service

RESERVATIONS
Not accepted

CREDIT CARDS
Not accepted

À LA CARTE
160–185AS

FIXED-PRICE MENU
None

SERVICE
Service included

ENGLISH
Yes

(10) FLAMMÓH
A-1010, Hohenstaufengasse 2

Flammóh is an old Viennese word meaning "I'm hungry," and you will need to be if you eat here. Anytime you come, for breakfast, lunch, or dinner, you are likely to be the only tourist. There isn't an official breakfast menu, but owner Dina Löffler says, "Just ask and we will prepare it for you." Perhaps an omelette or a plate of ham and eggs. For lunch there are at least four or five main-course salads ranging from an Indian curry affair (starring pineapple, pickles, ham, and greens) to tuna or shrimp. Paired with a cup of her special liver

TELEPHONE
533 70 92

U-BAHN
2, Schottentor

OPEN
Mon–Fri

CLOSED
Sat–Sun, holidays

HOURS
Breakfast 9–11 A.M., regular menu 11:30 A.M.–10 P.M., continuous service

RESERVATIONS
Suggested

dumpling soup, this makes a filling meal. Other lunch or dinner suggestions include warm turkey served with a side salad, fresh fish, or pepper steak. All the desserts are made here, and I recommend a sweet omelette or the pancakes with strawberry sauce and mounds of whipped cream.

(11) GIGERL
A-1010, Rauhensteingasse 3, entrance at Blumenstockgasse 2

Go to Gigerl for the wine and the music. For the best experience, arrive later in the evening, at least after 8 P.M., when the Austrian country music—complete with violin, guitar, and accordian—hits its stride.

This is a place with hard seats and benches, communal tables, lots of smoke, and no gourmet surprises. Cheap Eaters will concentrate on the buffet, which is priced by the weight of the individual dishes and available until midnight. À la carte is served only until 10 P.M.

(12) GULASCHMUSEUM
A-1010, Schulerstrasse 20

With a menu printed in five languages and many of the goulash dishes shown in colorful photos, this place clearly depends on tourists for the bulk of its trade. But that isn't all bad, and if you remember to stick to one of the nine or more renditions of this Austro-Hungarian favorite, you will be fine. There is a Monday to Friday lunch menu geared for office workers who want something cheap, filling, and fast, but you should skip this. Only order the goulash, which comes in a variety of ways and is served in he-man portions. Unless you are a marathon runner, this will be *the* meal of the day. You have a choice of beef, smoked pork, chicken liver, turkey, or pepper sausage goulash, garnished with dumplings and potatoes. Non–meat eaters can order either a fish or mushroom goulash. Best seating is in the small main room, dominated by a bar in the middle and banquette seating along the side.

À LA CARTE
95–120AS

FIXED-PRICE MENU
Lunch Mon–Fri, 85AS, 3 courses (no goulash)

SERVICE
Service included

ENGLISH
Yes, and menu in English

(13) GÖSSER BIERKLINIK ZUM GÜLDENEN DRACHEN
A-1010, Steindlgasse 4

Gösser Bierklinik, better known as Güldenen Drachen, has had a long and interesting history. The house, located in the oldest part of Vienna, was first mentioned in 1406. The next time history noted the house was in 1566, when it belonged to a shoemaker and for some reason was given the name Gülden Drache, or the Golden Dragon. In 1683 the house was given to Johann Steindl as a reward for defending Vienna. Steindl opened the house as an inn, and to this day it remains a place for eating and drinking. Since then over the years it has had a variety of colorful owners, including religious orders and the Goss brewery. It is now in the hands of a private owner.

When you reserve a table, ask for one in the main room, which has stained-glass windows, a skylight in the ceiling, and an old stone fireplace with a dragon perched on a shelf above it. Surrounding this room are several areas of booth seating, perfect for small groups. You definitely don't want to sit in the sterile upstairs room off the kitchen. If you just want a drink and light snack, go to the bar, just to the right as you enter. Here the atmosphere is more casual, but it can get smoky. In the main dining area, there is a designated nonsmoking section.

The menu is designed for carnivores with serious appetites. Noodles with mushrooms and slices of beef, chopped veal with dumplings and a cheese topping, venison with cranberries and dumplings, and turkey breast with herb sauce, broccoli, and rice are just a few of the selections. For dessert, I love the gingerbread with white chocolate sauce, colorfully accented with tangerines, or the poppyseed-filled pancake.

TELEPHONE
535 6897

U-BAHN
1, 3, Stephansplatz or 3, Herrengasse

OPEN
Mon–Sat

CLOSED
Sun, holidays, Dec 24–27, Jan 1–8

HOURS
11:30 A.M.–11:30 P.M., continuous service

RESERVATIONS
Suggested

CREDIT CARDS
MC, V

À LA CARTE
190–275AS

FIXED-PRICE MENU
None

SERVICE
10% service added to bill

ENGLISH
Yes, and menu in English

MISCELLANEOUS
Dining room has nonsmoking section

(14) KÖNIGSBACHER
A-1010, Walfischgasse 5

TELEPHONE
513 12 10

U-BAHN
1, 2, 4, Karlsplatz

OPEN
Mon–Fri; Sat lunch only

CLOSED
Sun, holidays

HOURS
Mon–Fri 10:30 A.M.–
11:30 P.M., continuous service;
Sat 10:30 A.M.–4 P.M.

RESERVATIONS
Essential

CREDIT CARDS
AE, V

À LA CARTE
120–180AS

FIXED-PRICE MENU
Lunch Mon–Fri, 95AS, 2 courses

SERVICE
Service discretionary

ENGLISH
Yes

You can't beat the location, just off the busy Kärntner Strasse and near the Opera. The dining room has leather-upholstered seats and dark, half-timbered walls, but in the summer, ask for a table outside on the terrace, which is just far enough away from the traffic on Kärntner Strasse to keep it pleasant. In addition to the weekly two-course lunch menu, which offers a soup and a warm dish, or a large salad in the summer, there is a monthly à la carte menu. In late fall, look for baked eggplant with mozzarella cheese, spinach *Nudel* (noodles) with butter and parmesan, or veal with tart red berries similar to cranberries.

Dessert might be a fruit strudel with whipped cream or a sweet cheese strudel. Wines are featured by the glass or the bottle. The owners, an attractive mother and daughter team, greet their regular guests and see that everyone receives a cordial welcome and good service.

(15) LUSTIG ESSEN
A-1010, Salvatorgasse 6

TELEPHONE
533 03 37

U-BAHN
1, 4, Schwedenplatz

OPEN
Daily

CLOSED
Never

HOURS
11:30 A.M.–midnight,
continuous service

RESERVATIONS
Not necessary

CREDIT CARDS
Not accepted

À LA CARTE
80–160AS

FIXED-PRICE MENU
None

SERVICE
10AS cover, service discretionary

ENGLISH
Yes, and menu in English

MISCELLANEOUS
Restaurant will issue only one bill per table

Fed up with huge portions of meat garnished with nothing more colorful than a boiled potato and a dumpling? If so, read on.

In terms of atmosphere, Lustig essen scores a big zero. But on the scale of Cheap Eats, it gets high marks. The concept here is appetizer-size dishes, all individually priced and changed on a daily, weekly, and monthly basis. This allows diners to try a variety of Austrian and European dishes without blowing both the waistline and the budget. For instance, for either lunch or dinner you could start with a serving of ham stuffed with mascarpone, a garlic cream soup, or spinach dumplings with a zucchini ragout. Next, saltimbocca (veal fillet) with prosciutto and dumplings, turkey goulash, or boiled beef with horseradish and potatoes. Vegetarians are well cared for with numerous salads, broccoli gratinée, and veggie burgers with tartar sauce. Desserts include chocolate fondue for two, crêpes suzettes with vanilla ice cream and almonds, and a tarte. There are at least five or six choices for every course, and because they are small, everyone can order several and then sample all the fare.

(16) MÖVENPICK
Ringstrassengalerien
A-1010, Kärntner Strasse

Mövenpick has something for everyone, including the most imaginative bathrooms in Vienna. This restaurant-*marché* is housed in the glittering Ringstrassen-galerien on the Kärntner Strasse. From babies to grannies, everyone will find something they like at this cafeterialike place. Before deciding, cruise the entire area and look at the salad bar, the pizza and pasta stations, the hot main dishes, the delicious desserts, and the wonderful ice cream. Then, this is the drill: go to whatever food stations have the food you want. There, servers will dole out your portion, you'll pay at a cashier, and then you'll take your tray to one of the tables positioned around the large space. There are tables for nonsmokers, those with play areas for children, and others perfectly positioned for people-watching.

Before you leave—or even if you are just passing through and have no intention of eating—stop by the ladies' bathroom, which is well worth the five shillings it costs to use it. There are four stalls, each one named after a man. One has a pair of old shoes peeking out; another is papered with photos of famous actors. I can't vouch for the men's room, but if you see it, let me know.

TELEPHONE
512 50 06

U-BAHN
1, 2, 4, Karlsplatz

OPEN
Daily

CLOSED
Never

HOURS
Mon–Sat 9 A.M.–9 P.M., Sun 11 A.M.–9 P.M., continuous service

RESERVATIONS
Not necessary

CREDIT CARDS
AE, DC, MC, V

À LA CARTE
Coffee and cake 40AS, full meal 150AS

FIXED-PRICE MENU
None

SERVICE
Service included

ENGLISH
Yes

(17) NASCHMARKT
A-1010, Freyung, Schottengasse 1

The man standing in the cafeteria queue next to me was holding a Filene's Basement Bag with the words "I Just Got a Bargain." He was in line for another great one at this stepped-up soup kitchen, which has two locations and feeds everyone in Vienna from the down-and-out to dowagers in mink, from pensioners to the young and the restless. Go early to get the best selection and the freshest food.

The Cheap Eating deals are definitely the daily special menus, which feature soup, main course, and a simple dessert of either fruit, pudding, or cake. The self-service dining rooms are very pleasant, with nice seating, good light, no-smoking sections, and plenty of Cheap Eats in Vienna worth repeating.

NOTE: There is a second Naschmarkt (17a on the map) at A-1010, Schwarzenbergplatz 16; telephone: 505 31 15. Take the U-Bahn to Karlsplatz (lines 1, 4).

TELEPHONE
533 51 86

U-BAHN
2, Schottentor

OPEN
Daily

CLOSED
Never

HOURS
Mon–Fri 10:30 A.M.–7:30 P.M., Sat until 5 P.M., Sun until 3 P.M., continuous service

RESERVATIONS
Not accepted

CREDIT CARDS
Not accepted

À LA CARTE
Salads 25AS, full meals 90AS

FIXED-PRICE MENU
Lunch or dinner, 70AS, 3 courses, no choices

SERVICE
Service included

ENGLISH
Very limited, but it won't matter

MISCELLANEOUS
Nonsmoking section

(18) OFENLOCH $
A-1010, Kurrentgasse 8

TELEPHONE
533 88 44

U-BAHN
1, 3, Stephansplatz

OPEN
Daily

CLOSED
A few days at Christmas

HOURS
11:30 A.M.–midnight,
continuous service

RESERVATIONS
Essential

CREDIT CARDS
AE, DC, MC, V

À LA CARTE
300–325AS

FIXED-PRICE MENU
Lunch Mon–Fri, 100–165AS, 3
courses

SERVICE
25AS cover (no cover in first
room), service discretionary

ENGLISH
Yes, and menu in English

Ask any Viennese resident to name his or her five favorite restaurants in the city, and most likely Ofenloch will be on the list. As with many buildings in this old part of the city, its history goes way back. From the first to the fourth centuries, a Roman palace stood here. By the thirteenth century, it had become a bathouse in the Jewish Quarter, and later it was a house of public welfare established by a Jewish brotherhood. In 1697 a Jewish food stall opened in the building, and by 1704 Ofenloch beer house was going strong, as it has continued to this day. If you ask, someone will be happy to point out the piece of old brick still in tact from the beginning of the first century.

Naturally charm and atmosphere are in high order, and on top of all that, the food is good. The many small rooms display original carved paneling, lovely murals, and unusual lights by the bar. Waitresses in long aprons pass out menus in newspaper form. While at first it may appear to be rather expensive, if you go for the fixed-price lunch, you can stay within a Cheap Eat budget. Many of the dishes are liberally garnished, assorted salads will be plenty for light eaters, and vegetarians will always find something to please. For a full meal, start with the puff pastry filled with goat cheese or the potato and mushroom soup. Follow this by a veal or pork schnitzel or leg of lamb with thyme sauce. For dessert, I like the apple strudel or, for something quite typical but on the heavy side, chestnut and nougat dumplings with strawberry sauce.

(19) PANTHER BRÄU
A-1010, Judenplatz 9–10

TELEPHONE
533 44 26

U-BAHN
1, 3, Stephansplatz

OPEN
Mon–Fri

CLOSED
Sat–Sun, holidays

HOURS
9:30 A.M.–11 P.M., continuous
service

RESERVATIONS
Not necessary

CREDIT CARDS
Not accepted

At lunch, which is the best time to sample this restaurant, your dining companions will be a mix of office workers and businessfolk. They are an uncritical audience, coming mainly for the Cheap Eat lunch menu, which changes daily and offers a soup and a garnished main course. All the standbys are also available à la carte: smoked meat platters with mounds of sauerkraut and dumplings, roast beef, and pork with onions and browned potatoes. The menu also leans heavily on dishes most Americans shun, but if you are game, order one— you will probably be pleasantly surprised. Here is your chance to try deep-fried brains, roast kidneys, or liver, breaded and deep-fried; all are garnished with potatoes or a mixed salad. Service is friendly and swift, especially at lunch. While waiting for your food, sample one of the pretzel bread twists hanging on the rack in the middle of your table. They are delicious; just know that you will be charged a few extra shillings for the pleasure.

À LA CARTE
110–195 AS

FIXED-PRICE MENU
Lunch, 65 AS, 2 courses

SERVICE
Service included

ENGLISH
Some, and menu in English

(20) PÜRSTNER $
A-1010, Riemergasse 10

The old brick floors, painted ceilings, and pretty Austrian tablecloths create a warm and cozy atmosphere at Pürstner. Candles burning at night and pillows tossed on the wooden booth benches add to the appealing scene. When reserving your table, ask for one under the half-barrel archways, or one in the back room by the fireplace. The menu is a well-thought-out presentation featuring weekly specials and, from October to December, seasonal game dishes. In addition, five different preparations of steak range from the familiar pepper steak to a calorie-infused slab of beef covered with ham, mushrooms, and cheese sauce. For dessert, there are the usual cheese and apple strudels, or for something slighly guilt-free, yogurt with fresh fruit and pistachios.

TELEPHONE
512 63 57

U-BAHN
1, 3, Stephansplatz or 3, Stubentor

OPEN
Daily

CLOSED
Christmas Eve

HOURS
11 A.M.–midnight, continuous service

RESERVATIONS
Suggested

CREDIT CARDS
AE, DC, MC, V

À LA CARTE
225–300 AS

FIXED-PRICE MENU
None

SERVICE
15% service added to bill

ENGLISH
Yes

(21) ROSENBERGER MARKTRESTAURANT
A-1010, Führichgasse 3

The Cheap Eating possibilities at the Rosenberger Marktrestaurant are varied. First, there is the self-serve bistro and bar on the street level, which is a good place for a quick coffee. For something more substantial, take the glass elevator down two flights to the large area dotted with a dozen or so food stations. Check out the entire operation before making a final food commitment. Choices include fresh fruit and vegetable juices, soup, salad, pastas, waffles topped with fruit and/or whipped cream, and main dishes such as chicken and rice, pork roast with vegetables, and sausages. And don't forget the desserts, which are all tempting. After making your selection, pay at the cashier and take your plate

TELEPHONE
512 34 58

U-BAHN
1, 2, 4, Karlsplatz

OPEN
Daily

CLOSED
Never

HOURS
Bistro and shop, 7:30 A.M.–11 P.M.; restaurant, 10:30 A.M.–11 P.M., continuous service

RESERVATIONS
Not accepted

CREDIT CARDS
AE, DC, MC, V

À LA CARTE
Coffee 25 AS, 3-course meal 120 AS

to any table; there are even some reserved for nonsmokers. When you are finished, stroll through the gift store upstairs, which features packaged goodies perfect for taking back to your hotel for a midnight snack.

(22) SPECHT
A-1010, Bäckerstrasse 12

If you don't have time to visit one of the wine garden restaurants outside of Vienna, this modern adaptation of a Grinsing *Heuriger* (wine garden) in back of St. Stephen's Cathedral is a good option. Austrian wines by the glass, pitcher, or bottle are served along with the usual buffet of hot and cold foods, which are designed to provide sustenance during an evening of drinking. That is, think breaded and fried for most of the hot meat and vegetables. Friday and Saturday nights include live violin and accordian music.

(23) STADTBEISL $
A-1010, Naglergasse 21

Centuries ago Stadtbeisl was a monestary where a Hungarian order of nuns fed soup and bread to the poor in Vienna. Underneath are catacombs, which the owner, Reinhard Proksch, will show you if he is here and has the time. The restaurant itself has an inviting mixture of dark wood in the rather informal first room, set with five booths around bare tables, and a hunter's room in the back with its original ceramic fireplace. In the summer, there is a pleasant garden.

Waiters in Austrian jackets serve traditional Viennese cuisine. The regular menu is long and timeless. Frankly I ignore it altogether and ask for the *Tageskarte*, or daily menu, which features the best the market and the chef have to offer. True, it is all in German, but the waiters are gracious and will patiently help you with your selections. In the fall and winter, wild game is a highlight. Otherwise, stick with one of the veal preparations or a filling pork dish, liberally garnished with onions and potatoes. Strudels, *Mohr im Hemd*—a chocolate bundt cake served with ice cream and double whipped cream—and pancakes with chocolate sauce and whipped cream, of course, guarantee dieter dispair.

(24) STOPFER
A-1010, Rudolfsplatz 4

Consistency and home cooking are the bywords at Stopfer, a family-owned place where mother and son run the kitchen and a friendly staff greet and serve the many neighborhood regulars, who almost consider it home. It is the sort of spot where daily card games are played, and the bar is dotted with drinkers who can be counted on to show up at their usual time every day. The dining room is simple, bright, and cheery with knotty pine and pink and green table linens.

If you like liver, try the roasted pork liver served with mushrooms. Another favorite is roast beef smothered in onions and potatoes. At lunch Cheap Eaters can always count on a garnished blue-plate special. Perhaps it will be lasagna, turkey, or a large salad filled with meat and cheese. Desserts display the usual Viennese disregard for calories. However, you can be somewhat frugal on this score with the vanilla ice cream covered with berries, or maybe share the *Topfenpalatschinken,* a sweet cheese pancake.

TELEPHONE
533 64 62
U-BAHN
2, Schottentor
OPEN
Mon–Fri
CLOSED
Sat–Sun; holidays, Dec 24–Jan 7, Aug 1–24
HOURS
9 A.M.–11 P.M., continuous service
RESERVATIONS
Suggested for dinner
CREDIT CARDS
Not accepted
À LA CARTE
130–175AS
FIXED-PRICE MENU
Lunch blue-plate special, 75–90AS
SERVICE
Service discretionary
ENGLISH
Yes, and menu in English

(25) TRZEŚNIEWSKI
A-1010, Dorotheergasse 1

For one of the Cheapest Eats in Vienna, head for Trześniewski and order the only thing they serve: open-face sandwiches, with more than twenty toppings to choose from. Each one costs the same—only 10AS—and they are small, so choose several, which the server will put on a plate. Then you pay, get a prepaid disk for your beer, and try to nab a stand-up spot at one of the counters—or if you are lucky, a seat at the bench along the side. They also do take-away if you don't want to fight the crowd.

TELEPHONE
512 32 91
U-BAHN
1, 3, Stephansplatz
OPEN
Mon–Sat
CLOSED
Sun, holidays
HOURS
Mon–Fri 8:30 A.M.–7:30 P.M., Sat 9 A.M.–5 P.M.
RESERVATIONS
Not accepted
CREDIT CARDS
Not accepted
À LA CARTE
All sandwiches 10AS each
FIXED-PRICE MENU
None
SERVICE
No service charged or expected
ENGLISH
Limited, but you won't need it

(26) WIENER PALATSCHINKEN PLATZL
A-1010, Grasshofgasse 4 (off Kollnerhofgasse)

TELEPHONE
513 82 18

U-BAHN
1, 4, Schwedenplatz

OPEN
Daily

CLOSED
Never

HOURS
10 A.M.–midnight, continuous service

RESERVATIONS
Not necessary

CREDIT CARDS
AE, DC, MC, V

À LA CARTE
80–150AS

FIXED-PRICE MENU
Lunch or dinner, 90AS and 100AS, 2 courses, no choices, no pancakes

SERVICE
No service charged or expected

ENGLISH
Yes, and menu in English

When you come to the original pancake house of Vienna, you order pancakes . . . what else? You also need to come with a big appetite because most servings consist of three stuffed pancakes. Specialties include those filled with chanterelle mushrooms, bacon, onions, and egg with an herb sauce; a rustic meatloaf, cheese, and egg pancake served with salad and tartar sauce; or one featuring spinach, ham, and cheese, topped with a fried egg. Three vegeterian selections include fillings of zucchini, black salsify, or gratinéed camembert, walnuts, and stewed cranberries.

Still haven't had enough? Then go for broke with either a browned omelette filled with apples, cinnamon, and sugar or one of the dessert pancakes, which come two or three to a plate. You can go the simple route and have yours with just jam, but why not indulge in one with sweet chestnuts and chocolate sauce, or with strawberries and curd, topped with vanilla crème? Aside from the thirty-plus pancakes, there are main-course salads, a variety of pastas, and even fried pork chops or goulash.

(27) WILD
A-1010, Neuer Markt 10–11

TELEPHONE
512 53 03

U-BAHN
1, 2, 4, Karlsplatsz or 1, 3, Stephansplatz

OPEN
Mon–Fri; Sat breakfast and lunch only

CLOSED
Sun, holidays

HOURS
Mon–Fri 8:30 A.M.–6:30 P.M., hot lunches noon–2 P.M.; Sat 8:30 A.M.–1 P.M.

RESERVATIONS
Not necessary

CREDIT CARDS
AE, DC, MC, V

À LA CARTE
Pastry 45AS, daily special 100AS

FIXED-PRICE MENU
None

SERVICE
No service charged or expected

ENGLISH
Limited

If you locate the vegetable and fruit stand on the square, you will have found this divine delicatessen, bakery, and wine shop, which serves wonderful hot meals at lunch during the week. If time is an issue, join the well-dressed clientele eating at the stand-up buffet. Otherwise, hope for a table and order whatever the special is for the day. The menu lists what the chef will be cooking for the next two weeks, so if you aren't in the mood for chili con carne today, you might like the pot roast tomorrow or the veal goulash on Friday. Bear in mind that the hot lunches are served only from noon until 2 P.M., but if you miss this, there is always a handcrafted sandwich from the deli.

(28) WRENKH $
A-1010, Bauernmarkt 10

Wrenkh is heaven's answer to the prayers of vegetarians marooned in Vienna. For almost two decades, this all-vegetarian fare has drawn a smart crowd looking for alternatives to meat, fat, sugar, and starch as dining staples. The imaginative menu changes every three or four weeks and highlights only first-rate, fresh ingredients. The service is attentive, and the seating in the up-to-date dining room, with its upholstered booths and black wood accents, is comfortable and relaxing.

Many of the appetizers, soups, and salads come in two sizes. I always like to start with a small mixed plate of their delicious starters, which could include their specialty, their version of tabbouleh: spicy bulgur wheat garnished with cucumber, parsley, and seasoned with garlic, lemon juice, and cayenne pepper. In the summer, look for the Styrian salad, which is a large green salad with white beans and sheep cheese in pumpkin seed oil. For the main course, you can always count on two long-standing favorite dishes: whole wheat *Spätzle*—which is Austrian egg pasta in a white wine and goat cheese sauce, served with spinach and mushrooms—or the zucchini risotto, dotted with onions and smoked tofu cubes and flavored with pumpkin seed oil and parmesan cheese. Winter menus feature potato patties with a carbonara sauce or the mushrooms à la crème, special Austrian mushrooms garnished with bread dumplings. Other favorites include *Potatoe Schmarrn*—minced, roasted potatoes served with vegetables in garlic butter and served with a cottage cheese sauce. In addition, there is a "Light and Tasty" section of the menu with one-dish meals, such as steamed fennel in a thyme-carrot sauce, served with millet, or the chef's own gnocchi with vegetables in a tomato sauce. For dessert you have seasonal choices such as mango cream, poppyseed noodles with honey butter, or the best choice of all, the dessert combination, which offers a bite or two of everything in the dessert lineup.

TELEPHONE
533 15 26

U-BAHN
1, 3, Stephansplatz

OPEN
Mon–Sat

CLOSED
Sun, holidays

HOURS
Bar (light snacks), 11 A.M.–midnight; restaurant, lunch noon–2 P.M., dinner 5:30–9 P.M.

RESERVATIONS
Suggested, especially for lunch

CREDIT CARDS
AE, DC, MC, V

À LA CARTE
Lunch or dinner 264–320AS, bar snacks 50–90AS

FIXED-PRICE MENU
None

SERVICE
Service included

ENGLISH
Yes, and menu in English

(29) ZUM SCHWARZEN KAMEEL $
A-1010, Bognergasse 5

The restaurant bears the name of Mr. Kameel, who came to Vienna from Brno in the Czech Republic and started a restaurant at this address in 1618. In 1902, it

TELEPHONE
533 81 25

U-BAHN
1, 3, Stephansplatz or 3, Herrengasse

Mon–Sat; restaurant Mon–Fri
for lunch only
CLOSED
Sun, holidays
HOURS
Bar, Mon–Fri 9 A.M.–8 P.M., Sat
9 A.M.–3 P.M., hot food in bar
Mon–Fri 3–8 P.M.; deli, Mon–
Fri 8:30 A.M.–7 P.M., Sat
8:30 A.M.–3 P.M.; restaurant,
lunch Mon–Fri noon–3 P.M.
RESERVATIONS
Essential for restaurant lunch
CREDIT CARDS
AE, DC, MC, V
À LA CARTE
Restaurant lunch 250–350AS;
deli sandwiches 15–38AS; bar
snacks 25–100AS
FIXED-PRICE MENU
None
SERVICE
Service included
ENGLISH
Yes

was redesigned by Adolf Loos, one of the most recognized designers in the Art Nouveau era. This very old house still bears his magnificent designs. For nearly the last five decades, it has been in the hands of the same family and is well known not only for its excellent food but for its wine cellars and catering service.

For the visitor in the heart of Vienna, it offers a place to have a glass of excellent wine or champagne and a bite to eat before going to the opera; a good place for a special lunch in the restaurant section; or a deli with a stand-up snack bar for a quick sandwich. The lunch menu in the dining room is rather short, and I like that. It tells me that the chef is concentrating on what is best at the moment and not relying on a freezer full of other possibilities. You will always find a beef, veal, and pork dish, attractive salads, and creamy desserts. On the deli side, beautiful sandwiches are popular lunch orders for those in a hurry, and in the evening, you can order food in the bar, organizing a light sampler plate of tempting selections before attending a theater performance.

Cafés

TELEPHONE
533 37 63
U-BAHN
3, Herrengasse
OPEN
Mon–Sat
CLOSED
Sun, holidays
HOURS
Café 8 A.M.–10 P.M., warm food
10 A.M.–7 P.M.; restaurant lunch
11:30 A.M.–3 P.M.
RESERVATIONS
Suggested for restaurant lunch
CREDIT CARDS
AE, DC, MC, V
À LA CARTE
Coffee from 40AS, pastries
45AS, café meal 50–200AS,
restaurant lunch 300–375AS
FIXED-PRICE MENU
Restaurant lunch only, 310AS,
3 courses
SERVICE
No service charged or
expected; in restaurant, service
discretionary
ENGLISH
Yes

(30) CAFÉ CENTRAL
A-1010, Herrengasse 14

At the turn of the century, artists, writers, and radicals met at this beautifully elegant Art Nouveau café, which is part of the Ferstel Palace. Here, poets Arthur Schnitzler and Peter Altenberg, critic Karl Kraus, architect Adolf Loos, and revolutionary Leon Trotsky ate, socialized, worked, and held court. Today it is still a favored meeting place for impassioned players who pursue the pastime of their choice, whether it be reading, arguing, playing chess, or just whiling away the afternoon.

The restaurant section, which is open only for lunch, is expensive by Cheap Eating standards, but a coffee and a pastry, or a light meal in the café section, can certainly be part of anyone's Vienna experience. If you arrive in the late afternoon, you will have the added bonus of live piano music.

(31) CAFÉ GREINSTEIDL
A-1010, Michaelerplatz 2

The Café Greinsteidl occupies a prime corner on Michaelerplatz, an elegant showpiece square that is home to ministries and embassies in Vienna. It is also where you go to attend a performance of the famous Lipizzaner horses at the Spanish Riding School. What you see today at the Café Greinsteidl is the 1990 restored version of the original café, which was torn down around the turn of the century. Globe lights, black bentwood chairs, and red velvet banquettes by the windows make up the large wraparound site, which is popular with nostalgia buffs. An added bonus for most Americans is the no-smoking section, which is almost unheard of in a Viennese café. The food is traditional, with smaller portions available for senior citizens.

TELEPHONE
535 26 92
U-BAHN
3, Herrengasse
OPEN
Daily
CLOSED
Never
HOURS
8 A.M.–midnight
RESERVATIONS
Not necessary
CREDIT CARDS
AE, DC, MC, V
À LA CARTE
Coffee from 40AS, pastries from 50AS, meals 220–285AS
FIXED-PRICE MENU
None
SERVICE
No service charged or expected
ENGLISH
Limited
MISCELLANEOUS
Nonsmoking section

(32) CAFÉ ENGLÄNDER
A-1010, Postgasse 2

For a local spot with absolutely zip in the decor category, Café Engländer is almost at the top of the list. It has been here for years, as evidenced by the ochre, smoke-aged walls and the crusty waiters, who seem to have come with the original building. Still, it is a worthy and interesting Cheap Eat where you will encounter a cross-section of Viennese life: from the old couple with their dog resting at their feet to the two wheeler-dealers in sunglasses talking in hushed tones into their cell phones. You can eat simply if you order the frankfurter with sauerkraut and a roll, an omelette, or a salad plate. Everything has a price tag, so watch what you order. If you pick up a portion of bread and only eat half, you will be charged for it all. While you are here, take a minute to look inside the beautiful church at Postgasse 6 and admire its ornate frescoed ceiling.

TELEPHONE
512 27 34
U-BAHN
1, 4, Schwedenplatz
OPEN
Daily
CLOSED
Never
HOURS
Mon–Sat 8 A.M.–1 A.M., Sun 11 A.M.–midnight
RESERVATIONS
Not necessary
CREDIT CARDS
AE, DC, MC, V
À LA CARTE
Coffee from 38AS, meals 75–250AS
FIXED-PRICE MENU
Lunch or dinner, 110AS, 120AS, and 140AS, 2 courses, no choices
SERVICE
No service charged or expected
ENGLISH
Yes

(33) CAFÉ FRAUENHUBER
A-1010, Himmelpfortgasse 6

TELEPHONE
512 43 23

U-BAHN
1, 2, 4, Karlsplatz or 1, 3,
Stephansplatz

OPEN
Daily

CLOSED
Never

HOURS
Mon–Sat 8 A.M.–midnight, Sun
10 A.M.–10 P.M.

RESERVATIONS
Not necesssary

CREDIT CARDS
Not accepted

À LA CARTE
Coffee from 40AS, breakfast
from 70AS, light meal 45–
100AS, full meal 200–220AS

FIXED-PRICE MENU
Lunch, 90AS, 2 courses, no choices

SERVICE
No service charged or expected

ENGLISH
Yes

Café Frauenhuber has the reputation of being a quiet, dignified meeting place with waiters providing proper service. The turn-of-the century interior seats everyone from young mothers with their babies in strollers to elderly ladies out for their afternoon coffee and pastry. The food is typical, and as in all cafés, you will not be treated rudely if you only order a salad or a bowl of soup.

(34) CAFÉ HAWELKA
A-1010, Dorotheergasse 6

TELEPHONE
512 82 30

U-BAHN
1, 3, Stephansplatz

OPEN
Mon, Wed–Sun

CLOSED
Tues

HOURS
Mon, Wed–Sat 8 A.M.–2 A.M.,
Sun 4 P.M.–2 A.M.

RESERVATIONS
Not necessary

CREDIT CARDS
Not accepted

À LA CARTE
Coffee from 10AS, snacks 40AS

FIXED-PRICE MENU
None

SERVICE
Service included

ENGLISH
Yes

Entire books have been written about Café Hawelka, which remains the epitome of the dark, smoky Viennese coffeehouse where the regulars sit for hours drinking coffee and smoking strong cigarettes. This place has been a fixture on the café circuit since it opened in 1900 as the first American bar in Vienna. In 1939 it was taken over by the Hawelka family, and it is run today by Günter Hawelka, the son. After the end of World War II, it became home to many Austrian writers and painters, some of whom paid their tabs with the paintings you see hanging on the walls. Atmosphere and a sense of times gone by are the strong points at Hawelka—the food is not. Ham and eggs, sandwiches, sausages, and their famous *Buchtel*—a sweet roll served only at night— are the only choices on the menu.

(35) CAFÉ LANDTMANN
A-1010, Dr. Karl Lueger Ring 4

Café Landtmann's magnificent building, lovely garden terrace, and location across from the Burgtheater make it one of the most popular meeting places in Vienna. Its history dates back to 1873, and it claims many famous customers, including Sigmund Freud. The menu has something for everyone at any time of day, and all the pastries are made here.

TELEPHONE
532 06 21

U-BAHN
2, Rathaus

OPEN
Daily

CLOSED
Never

HOURS
8 A.M.–midnight, breakfast 8–11:30 A.M., fixed-price lunch noon–2 P.M.

RESERVATIONS
Not necessary

CREDIT CARDS
AE, DC, MC, V

À LA CARTE
Coffee from 40AS, light meal 100–200AS

FIXED-PRICE MENU
Lunch Mon–Sat only, 110AS, 2 courses

SERVICE
No service charged or expected

ENGLISH
Yes, and menu in English

(36) CAFÉ MOZART
A-1010, Albertinaplatz 2

If you come to Café Mozart for a full à la carte meal, you will not have a Cheap Eat in Vienna. This is no different than most of the beautiful, old cafés that have histories spanning several centuries. However, no trip to Vienna would be complete without spending an hour or so in one, enjoying a coffee and light snack, and Café Mozart is a quiet, calm choice, with the view from the seats facing the Albertinaplatz worth the price of your café *Mokka*.

TELEPHONE
513 08 01

U-BAHN
1, 2, 4, Karlsplatz

OPEN
Daily

CLOSED
Never

HOURS
8 A.M.–midnight, breakfast 8–11:30 A.M.

RESERVATIONS
Not necessary

CREDIT CARDS
AE, DC, MC, V

À LA CARTE
Coffee from 40AS, Continental breakfast 80–135AS, meal 100–200AS

FIXED-PRICE MENU
None

SERVICE
Service included

ENGLISH
Yes, and menu in English

(37) KLEINES CAFÉ
A-1010, Franziskanerplatz 3

TELEPHONE
None

U-BAHN
1, 3, Stephansplatz

OPEN
Daily

CLOSED
Never

HOURS
Mon–Sat 10 A.M.–2 A.M.,
Sun 1 P.M.–2 A.M.

RESERVATIONS
Not accepted

CREDIT CARDS
Not accepted

À LA CARTE
Coffee 22–45 AS, sandwiches
30–50 AS, meals 30–95 AS

FIXED-PRICE MENU
None

SERVICE
Service included

ENGLISH
Yes

Located on a little square around the corner from Sotheby's, Kleines Café enjoys an almost continuous popularity all day and into the night. It is a friendly place where you can't make a reservation but are instead expected to share a table. For most of the day it is your typical coffeehouse, with the morning regulars glancing through the stacks of international newspapers and drinking coffee. When lunch rolls around, you'll need a shoehorn to get into the two tiny multicolored rooms. This is the time when the whole neighborhood stops by for one of their famous open-face sandwiches made on dark bread and piled high with ham and cheese, egg salad, or tomatoes and cucumbers. In the afternoon it is a good spot to spend an hour at one of the tufted red banquettes and admire the architecture by Hermann Czech. By 7 P.M. the tempo switches from coffeehouse to bar with loud sixties and seventies music and a black-outfitted under-thirty crowd who come to drink, mingle, meet, and mix . . . not to seriously eat. Breakfast can be served at midnight if you want it.

Tearooms and Pastry Shops

(38) AIDA
A-1010, Stephansplatz

TELEPHONE
Not available

U-BAHN
1, 3, Stephansplatz

OPEN
Daily

CLOSED
Never

HOURS
8 A.M.–9 P.M.

RESERVATIONS
Not accepted

CREDIT CARDS
Not accepted

À LA CARTE
Pastries from 25 AS

FIXED-PRICE MENU
None

SERVICE
No service charged or expected

ENGLISH
Enough

With more than two dozen locations in central Vienna, you will never be far from an Aida bakery. Open daily, they offer everything you could possibly want in pastries, light lunches, and snacks. In addition, there are chairs and tables where you can sit and be served. The quality is very high, the prices sensible, and the calorie-loaded pastries worth all the guilt.

(39) DEMEL'S
A-1010, Kohlmarkt 14

Enjoying a pastry at Demel's is as much a part of a trip to Vienna as visiting St. Stephen's Cathedral, attending a performance of the Vienna Boys Choir, or watching the famed Lipizzaner horses strut through their paces during a morning training session at the Spanish Riding School. However, no one ever said it was cheap.

Since its opening in 1786, Demel's has been considered *the* place to go in Vienna for the finest pastries, confections, ice creams, and sweets. The Emperor Franz Josef I had the shop's delicacies delivered to his palace, and no court ball, noble house party, or social event of any importance took place without sweets and ice creams from Demel's. In 1888 Demel's moved to the elegant Kohlmarkt location it occupies today. The rooms, in their ornate rococo style, are the same today, with the elegantly beautiful addition of the glass-enclosed Wintergarden. The exquisite Demel's products are still made by hand, and the beautiful packaging and show window designs are among the highlights of Vienna. In addition to the glorious array of sweet delights, Demel's serves tea sandwiches and light lunches, and it offers a salad and lunch buffet in the Wintergarden.

Chocolate lovers will want to join the *Sachertorte* debate by comparing Demel's delicious version with the original served only at the Hotel Sacher. *Sachertorte* was created in 1832 at the request of Prince Metternich, who wanted a very special dessert. His regular chef was not available, so the task of creating a princely dessert fell to a young apprentice named Franz Sacher. In 1876, his son Eduard opened the Hotel Sacher across from the Vienna Opera House. For reasons unknown, he sold the recipe for *Sachertorte* to the Demel family. It wasn't until 1950 that the legal battle began over who had the right to the original recipe. The final outcome: Hotel Sacher serves the "Original *Sachertorte*" with a round stamp in the center of the chocolate glaze, and the cake sliced showing a layer of jam. Demel's serves the "Original Eduard *Sachertorte*," with a triangular stamp and the jam under the glaze of the uncut cake.

TELEPHONE
535 17 17

U-BAHN
1, 3, Stephansplatz or 3, Herrengasse

OPEN
Daily

CLOSED
Never

HOURS
10 A.M.–7 P.M.

RESERVATIONS
Yes, for the Wintergarden

CREDIT CARDS
AE, MC, V

À LA CARTE
Pastries from 60AS, sandwiches 35–50AS, hot lunch 65–160AS, Wintergarden buffet 85–200AS

FIXED-PRICE MENU
None

SERVICE
Service included

ENGLISH
Yes

(40) KURKONDITOREI OBERLAAEN
A-1010, Neuer Markt 16

TELEPHONE
513 29 36

U-BAHN
1, 2, 4, Karlsplatz or 1, 3,
Stephansplatz

OPEN
Daily

CLOSED
Never

HOURS
Mon–Fri 8 A.M.–7 P.M., Sat
8 A.M.–6 P.M., Sun
10 A.M.–6 P.M.

RESERVATIONS
Not necessary

CREDIT CARDS
Not accepted

À LA CARTE
Breakfast 55–95AS, pastries
from 40AS

FIXED-PRICE MENU
Lunch, 100AS, 2 courses

SERVICE
No service charged or expected

ENGLISH
Enough

Open from breakfast through lunch and teatime, this wonderful pastry shop offers cakes, confections, and light lunches served on pretty china. One look at the seductive pastries artfully arranged in the glass case and you will know this is one eating pleasure in Vienna not to be missed.

(41) L. HEINER
A-1010, Kärntner Strasse 21–23

TELEPHONE
512 23 43

U-BAHN
1, 2, 4, Karlsplatz

OPEN
Daily

CLOSED
Never

HOURS
Mon–Sat 8:30 A.M.–7 P.M., Sun
10 A.M.–7 P.M.

RESERVATIONS
Not necessary

CREDIT CARDS
MC, V

À LA CARTE
Pastries from 40AS, light
lunches from 65AS

FIXED-PRICE MENU
None

SERVICE
No service charged or expected

ENGLISH
Yes

MISCELLANEOUS
Nonsmoking section

Three doors down from the American Express office on the Kärntner Strasse is this pastry shop (downstairs) and tearoom (upstairs) with plenty of delicious decisions to entice even the most die-hard dieter. There are a few tables by the pastry counter on the street level, and a mirrored, quiet no-smoking room is also here. The upstairs room is light and airy, with the best seats along the window facing the busy pedestrian promenade. During holiday times, the windows are spectacular, especially at Christmas when the gingerbread and marzipan confections attract wide-eyed onlookers of all ages.

OUTSIDE THE INNER RING _____

Near Belvedere Palace

Belvedere Palace is made up of two magnificent Baroque palaces separated by gardens. It originally was the summer palace of Prince Eugene of Savoy, and later was the home of the Archduke Franz Ferdinand, whose assassination in 1914 started World War I. Today, the upper palace displays a stunning collection of paintings by Egon Schiele, Gustav Klimt, and Oskar Kokoschka. The one-story lower palace houses paintings by leading Austrian painters of the seventeenth and eighteenth centuries.

RESTAURANTS

Restaurants

(42) SALM BRÄU
A-1030, Rennweg 8

After a workout at the Belvedere, you will probably be ready to relax and sit for awhile. A good place to do that is at the Salm Bräu, a microbrewery offering a changing selection of their own beers on tap, nonalcoholic bottled beers, wines, spirits, and schnapps. Seating is varied, and usually depends on the time of day and season. In warm weather, there is a terrace. During the day you will probably be seated on the main level, but in the evening you may be taken to the much more atmospheric cellar, which was once the wine cellar for the palace and later the stables. Food ranges from specialty salads and sandwiches big enough for two to goulash with potatoes, fried black pudding with cabbage pickled in beer, and the specialty of the house, salted haunch of ham, served with mustard and horseradish and guaranteed to feed at least two stevedores.

TELEPHONE
799 59 92

TRANSPORTATION
4, Stadpark, then Tram 71

OPEN
Daily

CLOSED
Christmas and New Year's Day

HOURS
11 A.M.–11 P.M., continuous service

RESERVATIONS
Not necessary

CREDIT CARDS
V

À LA CARTE
80–160AS, sandwiches 45–60AS

FIXED-PRICE MENU
Lunch, 70–90AS, 2 courses

SERVICE
Service included

ENGLISH
Yes, and menu in English

Josef Stadt and the Area Near the Rathaus

Other than the imposing Rathaus, Vienna's city hall, this area is pleasantly free of tourists. Josef Stadt is popular with students from the nearby universities. A stroll through these neighborhoods gives the visitor a good picture of everyday life in Vienna.

RESTAURANTS

TEAROOMS AND PASTRY SHOPS

A dollar sign ($) indicates a Big Splurge.

Restaurants

TELEPHONE
406 13 32

U-BAHN
2, Rathaus

OPEN
Daily; Sat–Sun dinner only

CLOSED
Between Christmas and New Year's, 2 weeks in Aug (dates vary)

HOURS
Mon–Fri 11:30 A.M.–midnight, Sat–Sun 5 P.M.–midnight

RESERVATIONS
Not necessary

CREDIT CARDS
AE, DC, MC, V

À LA CARTE
65–125AS

FIXED-PRICE MENU
Lunch, 80AS, either soup and a crêpe or a garnished meat dish

SERVICE
Service included

ENGLISH
Yes

(43) CRÊPERIE
A-1080, Schlösselgasse 8

Palatschinken are Austria's answer to the French crêpe, but what a difference a national border can make! *Palatschinken,* which are always huge, heavy, and filling, can be just too much for many visitors. If you are in the mood for a change of pace in Vienna, and are near the Rathaus, seek out Lotte Reiter's Crêperie, where the lighter French-style Breton crêpes come in sensible sizes and have either savory or sweet fillings.

Lotte has been here almost seventeen years, and her two-room restaurant looks much more French than Austrian. Her most popular main-course crêpes are those filled with spinach, ham, cheese, and egg; mushroom, tomato, cheese, and egg; and, believe it or not, blue cheese and applesauce. For dessert, order flambéed crêpes suzettes or a crêpe filled with caramel, apple, nuts, and honey. In keeping with the French theme of things, Beaujolais Nouveau is served in the late fall, and Breton cider is always available.

(44) GASTHAUS HUMMER
A-1080, Florianigasse 19

I lived for a time in this neighborhood, and I would see this simple corner location filled to capacity at lunch and throughout the day enjoying a steady stream of local drinkers, who remained unimpressed by the occasional visitor who strayed from the usual tourist trail and stumbled in. While certainly not destination nor gourmet dining, it is a place to remember for a glimpse of local color.

Obviously, the menu is too long for everything to be fresh. However, in season you can order deer fixed four ways: as goulash, steak, ragout, or sliced in a sauce. You can also touch base with all the central European favorites, such as garlic soup, sauerkraut with bratwurst, pork loin in pepper sauce, and beef pot roasts. I am not sure how high such things as stewed lungs and heart or chitterling dumplings with sour cabbage would rate, but they are available if you are brave enough to find out. For the vegetarian, there is precious little other than main dish salads or an omelette.

TELEPHONE
408 30 38

U-BAHN
2, Rathaus

OPEN
Mon–Fri, Sun in Oct–April;
Mon–Fri in May–Sept

CLOSED
Sat in Oct–April; Sat–Sun in
May–Sept

HOURS
Bar 9 A.M.–midnight; lunch
11:30 A.M.–3:30 P.M., dinner 5–
10 P.M.

RESERVATIONS
Not necessary

CREDIT CARDS
DC, MC, V

À LA CARTE
110–150AS

FIXED-PRICE MENU
Lunch, 60AS, soup and hot
plate

SERVICE
Service included

ENGLISH
Yes, and menu in English

(45) ORLANDO
A-1080, Florianigasse 20

Orlando is a homey Italian restaurant, run by a husband-and-wife team, where the first table by the front door might well be occupied by the owners' little boy working on a school project. As Italian restaurants go, it is really nothing remarkable, but it does serve up reliable standards to the neighborhood regulars who aren't in the mood to cook at home. The salads are all very fresh, and the pastas good, as long as you stay with something simple or with what the chef/husband proposes that day. Carafes of the house wine are drinkable.

A seaside theme is carried out with nets and shells hanging over the bar and in a mural along one wall. Tables are set with paper napkins and a lone candle in the evening, and the wife acts as hostess, waitress, and cashier. If it is crowded, expect some delays, as the food is made to order, and the husband and wife owners are the only staff.

TELEPHONE
408 47 41

U-BAHN
2, Rathaus

OPEN
Daily; Mon dinner only

CLOSED
Never

HOURS
Lunch Tues–Sun noon–3 P.M.,
dinner daily 6 P.M.–midnight

RESERVATIONS
Not necessary

CREDIT CARDS
Not accepted

À LA CARTE
140–175AS

FIXED-PRICE MENU
None

SERVICE
Service included

ENGLISH
Limited

(46) SCHNATTL $
A-1080, Lange Gasse 40

TELEPHONE
405 34 00

U-BAHN
2, Rathaus

OPEN
Mon–Fri; Sat dinner only

CLOSED
Sun; holidays, 2 weeks at Easter, 2 weeks in August, 3 days at Christmas

HOURS
Lunch Mon–Fri 11:30 A.M.–2:30 P.M., dinner Mon–Sat 6 P.M.–midnight

RESERVATIONS
Essential

CREDIT CARDS
AE, DC

À LA CARTE
340–400AS

FIXED-PRICE MENU
Lunch, 75AS, 2 courses, no choice

SERVICE
Service discretionary

ENGLISH
Yes

One of the best meals you can have in Vienna is at Schnattl. If you are watching your wallet, go for lunch and have the two-course lunch bargain. Otherwise, go for dinner and plan on an evening of dining pleasure. The green and black interior is plain yet elegant, with hurricane candles lit at night and service by tuxedo-clad waiters very correct. Try to avoid sitting in the first two rooms by reserving your table either in the main dining room or, during the summer, in the pretty garden. The owner/chef, Herr Schnattl, has been here more than ten years, and he has earned a well-deserved reputation as a creative, innovative chef. He does his own shopping at the market and changes his menu at least every two weeks.

In the late fall, his duck mousse, surrounded by slices of duck breast and a nut syrup, is a must. Other starters might include a mixed salad dressed in pumpkin oil or roasted blood sausages. He is famous for both his rosemary roasted rack of lamb and a richly rewarding calf's heart cooked like a roast beef and served with a Maderia wine sauce. Venison, rack of mountain goat, and guinea fowl round out the main courses at this time of year. Fortunately, the rack of lamb is usually available throughout the year, and so are fresh water and saltwater fish and a vegetarian main course. Desserts at Schnattl keep pace with the rest of the menu, especially the coconut souffle and, at Christmastime, his *Lebkuchen* (gingerbread) and his drunken *Stollen* in a light sauce. To round out this exceptional meal, treat yourself to a glass of schnapps—there are two pages of different types to choose from.

(47) TUNNEL
A-1080, Florianigasse 39

TELEPHONE
405 34 65

U-BAHN
2, Rathaus

OPEN
Daily

CLOSED
Never

HOURS
9 A.M.–2 A.M., continuous service; breakfast 9–11 A.M.; lunch special 11:30 A.M.–2:30 P.M.; hot food to 1:30 A.M.; live music nightly 8 P.M.–2 A.M.

If you've reached the age when you have to ask who the hottest rock bands are, Tunnel probably isn't for you. This is a real student dive, with two levels and a basement for live music at night. It is the sort of place where youth lounge for hours, never bothered by the mind-bending music or the appalling cast of smoke that hangs in the air. However, if you do know who's hip and who's not and are looking for some action in Vienna, you are sure to find it here. A monthly calendar lists the schedule of live music performances—by groups with names such as Mad Undertaker, Behind the Behind, and

Zoom. If you are going to be in town for any length of time and want to find out what's happening, stop by and hang out for awhile.

The food, which caters to vegetarians and vegans as well as carnivores, starts with five Cheap Eater friendly breakfasts served every day until 11 A.M. You have a choice of a big bowl of *Müsli* topped with yogurt and fruit; either a Spanish or ham omelette; a Continental breakfast enlarged with ham, salami, and fruit yogurt; and finally the Arab, featuring hummus, eggplant salad, and olives. The daily lunch specials are both meat-based and vegetarian, and so are all the pastas and pizzas, which are available from midday on.

(48) ZUR BÖHMISCHEN KUCHL
A-1080, Schlösselgasse 18

The neighborhood cognoscenti told me that this used to be a nothing place until Czech-born Herr Knizek took it over in the early nineties and transformed it into a charming memorial to the food and country lore of his homeland. The inside of the restaurant looks like an antique shop with wonderful collections of bottles, cups, mugs, and walking canes, along with ropes of hanging peppers, garlic braids, an old organ, stuffed game birds, and an entire wall dedicated to the first president of the Czech Republic, Tomáš Masaryk. An amusing sign by the bar states: "If I am drinking, my pocket is paying and my mother is filling my pockets with money." Somehow it all comes together to create a warm and cozy atmosphere in which to enjoy some delightful Czech and Bohemian cooking.

The house specialty is potato pancakes—and these you simply must try. They come nine different ways: simply flavored with garlic or bacon; served with scrambled eggs and cheese; enveloping smoked meat or a steak; garnishing a pork cutlet and topped with a fried egg; with turkey and a spicy paprika cream sauce; and gratinéed with cheese, ham, and onions. The rest of the menu is rather long, but has some real gems. Try the *svickova*, or Bohemian Wedding Dish, which is roasted beef with dumplings and a vegetable cream sauce and garnished with cranberries. If you order the *Svejk*—beef goulash—it comes garnished with sausage, a vegetable, and their famous potato pancakes. Lighter choices include homemade liver sausage served with cabbage salad, and pickled sausage in a vinaigrette sauce.

RESERVATIONS
Not necessary

CREDIT CARDS
Not accepted

À LA CARTE
30–150AS, breakfast 30AS

FIXED-PRICE MENU
Lunch, 48AS, one-plate meals

SERVICE
Service included

ENGLISH
Yes, and menu in English

TELEPHONE
402 57 31

U-BAHN
2, Rathaus

OPEN
Mon–Fri

CLOSED
Sat–Sun; holidays, 2 weeks between Christmas and New Year's, 2 weeks in summer (call to check)

HOURS
Lunch 11:30 A.M.–2:30 P.M., dinner 5:30–9:30 P.M.

RESERVATIONS
Suggested

CREDIT CARDS
Not accepted

À LA CARTE
125–175AS

FIXED-PRICE MENU
Lunch, 65AS, two menus with soup and hot dish

SERVICE
Service included

ENGLISH
Yes, and menu in English

Desserts are admittedly on the heavy side but are worth at least sharing, especially the *livance*, which consists of four *Palatschinken* (pancakes) filled with cream cheese and berry jam and buried in whipped cream. Slightly less filling, but just as typical, are the *Palatschinken* filled with red plum jam and dusted with poppyseeds. To top off your meal, sample one of the twenty-two *slivovice* (plum brandies), the Czech drink for special occasions, and at other times, too.

Tearooms and Pastry Shops

(49) DER MANN BÄCKEREI & KONDITOREI
A-1080, Alser Strasse 21

TELEPHONE
406 34 54
U-BAHN
2, Rathaus
OPEN
Mon–Sat
CLOSED
Sun, major holidays
HOURS
6:30 A.M.–8 P.M.
RESERVATIONS
Not accepted
CREDIT CARDS
Not accepted
À LA CARTE
Pastries from 10AS
SERVICE
No service charged or expected
ENGLISH
Enough

Der Mann rivals Aida for the number of locations in Vienna. The bakeries are always crowded, always good, and the prices are some of the lowest in the city. Everything is made in a central kitchen and brought to the individual shops to be baked. You can start the day with a poppyseed- or nut-filled sweet roll and a cup of strong coffee; stop in for a fat sandwich for lunch; grab a slice of cheese or apple strudel in the afternoon; and before they close pick up a loaf of bread or dessert for dinner later on. Though comfort and quiet relaxation over a coffee and pastry are not part of what Der Mann sells, most shops have a few small stand-up tables where you can eat your food.

(50) SLUKA
A-1010, Rathausplatz 8

Sluka has a well-deserved reputation as a reliable, dignified tearoom; it has been serving well-dressed children accompanied by their attractive mothers and stately grandmothers for generations.

It is rather small, with only twenty tables. The front area is where you sit if you are having a light snack or a pastry. Lunches are served in the second section, which is surrounded by banquettes. The tables in the middle are reserved for nonsmokers. In warm weather, the tables set outside are especially pleasant.

TELEPHONE
406 88 96
U-BAHN
2, Rathaus
OPEN
Mon–Sat
CLOSED
Sun, holidays
HOURS
Mon–Fri 8 A.M.–7 P.M., Sat 8 A.M.–5:30 P.M.
RESERVATIONS
Not necessary
CREDIT CARDS
MC, V
À LA CARTE
Pastries from 48AS, lunches from 75AS
FIXED-PRICE MENU
None
SERVICE
No service charged or expected
ENGLISH
Yes
MISCELLANEOUS
Nonsmoking section

Near Mariahilferstrasse, Spittelberg, and the Westbahnhof

In the sixteenth century, Spittelberg was nothing but vineyards outside the city walls. Later on, it became a place where prostitution ran rampant. Today, as you wander along the cobblestoned streets and peek into the old houses and courtyards, it is hard to imagine that the entire area was almost destroyed in the 1960s. However, due to hard work and perseverance by dedicated owners and businesspeople in the area, the delapidated houses with their beautiful Baroque and Biedermeier facades hidden behind centuries of dirt and neglect were restored to their original appearance. As you walk through the area, it is interesting to look at the names of some of the houses—such as, *Zum blauen Hechten,* the Blue Pike; *Zum schwarzen Rössl,* the Black Horse; and *Zum weissen Löwen,* the White Lion—and imagine what life was like in the district many years ago. Now it is a charming area filled with artists' boutiques, restaurants, and during the Christmas season, one of the best Christmas markets in the city.

Mariahilferstrasse serves as one of Vienna's most popular shopping streets. Both sides of the long street are lined with retail stores displaying goods for every price range and level of taste. To keep your energy level going strong there are numerous restaurants and fast-food options. The only reason a tourist would be around the Westbahnhof is to catch a train for the next destination.

RESTAURANTS

CAFÉS

A dollar sign ($) indicates a Big Splurge.

Restaurants

(51) CRÊPERIE-BRASSERIE SPITTELBERG
A-1070, Spittelberggasse 12

TELEPHONE
526 15 70

U-BAHN
2, 3, Volkstheater

OPEN
Daily

CLOSED
Never

HOURS
9 A.M.–midnight, continuous service

RESERVATIONS
Advised at night, especially on weekends and holidays

CREDIT CARDS
AE, DC, MC, V

À LA CARTE
Filled baguette 70AS, 3-course meal 200AS

FIXED-PRICE MENU
None

SERVICE
Service included

ENGLISH
Yes, and menu in English

Whenever I am in Spittelberg, I like to eat at Dr. Jürgen Stein's Crêperie-Brasserie. Dr. Stein deserves a great deal of the credit for the restoration and continuing development of Spittelberg. He opened his restaurant on a shoestring more than fifteen years ago, and he has since developed it into a favorite choice of his many regulars. The menu changes often and offers a range of French-inspired dishes guaranteed to fit into almost all budgets. It is possible to come for a baguette filled with goat cheese, spinach, and olives; order a pasta or the vegetarian dish of the day; dig into a *choucroute garnie,* a dish of pork cuts served with wine-flavored sauerkraut and potatoes; design your own small or large salad; enjoy a bowl of French onion soup topped with melted cheese; or order the specialties of the house—savory *galettes* made with buckwheat flour or sweet dessert crêpes made from wheat flour. The *galettes* come with a choice of at least eight combinations.The seven sweet dessert crêpes range from the Poirot, a compote of pears and cranberries with vanilla cream, to the Normandise, with apples, honey, raisins, nuts, and hazelnut liqueur.

(52) GASTHAUS SIEBOLD
A-1060, Aegidigasse 15 (at corner of Spalowskygasse)

If you like romantic stories, this one-hundred-year-old Gasthaus almost in the shadow of the Westbahnhof has a delightful one. It is the simple, heartwarming story of Inga and Gary Franceschi, and it adds a little something to the overall flavor of this out-of-the-way selection. A few years ago Inga was running the place by herself and raising her boys alone. Through the best friend of her sons, she met Gary, an American from San Francisco. Inga and Gary fell in love, and—you know the rest—were married and now run the Gasthaus together.

Quite frankly, unless someone told you about it, you would never even slow down as you passed by. However, its inviolate charms and dependably interesting clientele reflect blue-collar Vienna. For Cheap Eaters it is a godsend, especially the lunch deal, which costs less than the starters at many other places. If you are here at other times, the large portions are predictably authentic, especially if you stay with the first page of the menu. All of the cholesterol-infused dishes are here, from fried cheese served with an egg and French fries to schnitzels, blood sausages with fried potatoes and sauerkraut, and deep-fried chicken breast with a salad. Less health-threatening are the salad plates with ham, tuna, or cheese. For dessert, I recommend Inga's own apple strudel.

TELEPHONE
596 71 01

U-BAHN
3, 6, Westbahnhof

OPEN
Daily

CLOSED
Dec 24–Jan 6

HOURS
Mon–Fri 9 A.M.–11 P.M., Sat–Sun 11 A.M.–11 P.M., continuous service

RESERVATIONS
Not necessary

CREDIT CARDS
Not accepted

À LA CARTE
125–160AS

FIXED-PRICE MENU
Lunch Mon–Fri, 60AS, soup and main course, no choices

SERVICE
Service included

ENGLISH
Yes, and menu in English

(53) GASTHAUS WITWE BOLTE $
A-1070, Gutenberggasse 13

Spittelberg is an interesting and picturesque area of Vienna you should definitely visit. For many years, this was the city's "red light" district. Emperor Joseph II's mother, Maria Theresa, a strict and traditional Catholic, tried to stop the prostitution by instituting a chastity commission. The effort failed. When her son visited the area disguised as an ordinary citizen, he was thrown out of the Witwe Bolte, allegedly for his bad behavior. Proof of this can be found on one of the walls of the restaurant, where an inscription states just that: *Durch diese Tür in Bogen ist Kaiser Josef II, geflogen Anno 1787.*

The restaurant has appealing Old World decor spread through three wood-paneled rooms. Tables are set with linens and fresh flowers, and candles are added in the evenings. The beautiful garden in the summer attracts

TELEPHONE
523 14 50

U-BAHN
2, 3, Volkstheater

OPEN
Daily

CLOSED
Never

HOURS
Noon–midnight, continuous service

RESERVATIONS
Suggested on weekend evenings and holidays

CREDIT CARDS
DC, MC, V

À LA CARTE
300–350AS

many Viennese, who appreciate the dependability of the traditional food. Favorite dishes include *Boite Reindl,* slices of beef, veal, and pork in a mushroom sauce and served over buttered rice. Calf's liver in a juniper sauce is garnished with apples, and the traditional *Tafelspitz,* boiled beef rump, comes with carrots, sautéed potatoes, apples, and horseradish sauce. For dessert you can have the cream cheese dumplings with cranberries or, depending on your mood or dinner companion, the "hot love," which is a vanilla ice cream sundae topped with hot raspberries and whipped cream.

FIXED-PRICE MENU
None
SERVICE
Service included
ENGLISH
Usually, and menu in English

(54) SCHNIZELWIRT
A-1070, Neubaugasse 52

TELEPHONE
523 37 71
U-BAHN
3, Neubaugasse
OPEN
Mon–Sat
CLOSED
Sun, holidays
HOURS
11 A.M.–10 P.M., continuous service
RESERVATIONS
Not necessary
CREDIT CARDS
Not accepted
À LA CARTE
100–150AS
FIXED-PRICE MENU
Lunch, 70–80AS, garnished main course
SERVICE
No service charged or expected
ENGLISH
Yes

Purists claim that the only schnitzel worth having is one made from veal and cooked in a pan with butter— never, heaven forbid, deep fat fried. These schnitzel snobs don't eat here, but many others do, and happily. Cheap Eaters ranging from little old ladies out shopping with their tiny dogs to yuppies making cellular telephone calls during the meal come here to stoke up on the giant-size schnitzels that arrive at the table literally falling off the plate. Your choices include a hamburger schnitzel with fried potatoes; a Mexican version with smoked pork, peppers, and mushrooms; and for sumo wrestlers in training, the Holstein, roasted pork, fried eggs, rice, salad, and stewed fruit.

I can't imagine coming here and ordering anything other than schnitzel, but if you do, the omelettes are equally as large and filling. Unless the menu already states the garnishes, expect to pay extra for everything, even the ketchup, which will set you back an additional 5AS. Can you manage dessert? If so, think about the duet of jam- or chocolate-filled pancakes or a sweet omelette with stewed fruit. When you arrive, don't settle for any of the three tables by the entrance. Keep going to the back room.

(55) SIEBENSTERN BRÄU
A-1040, Siebensterngasse 19

TELEPHONE
523 86 97
U-BAHN
3, Neubaugasse
OPEN
Daily
CLOSED
Christmas

Renovation costs in excess of three million Austrian shillings restored one of the oldest buildings in Vienna's seventh district, known for its Biedermeier architecture. The tavern is one of the few private breweries in Vienna, and it offers a choice of five homemade brews dispensed directly "from the tanks straight into your glass." You can order *Prager Dunkles* (dark beer), *Wiener Helles* (pilsner), *Märzen* (pale beer), *Weizen* (wheat beer), and the house specialty, *Helles Mondscheinbier* (pale beer brewed at the full moon). The beers are brewed with the best hops and malt, and are billed as completely natural products without any chemical additives, thus preserving all the vitamins and nutrients. You can order other beers, take some home in one- or two-liter bottles, or tap your own beer from a barrel.

As you can imagine, this is the place to come with a group of like-minded beer-loving friends. There are seats for 480 drinkers, with 200 of them in the garden. Food? Did anyone mention food? Yes, they serve it, and in ample enough portions to keep you drinking for awhile. The best Cheap Eat is the Monday to Friday plate lunch, which changes every day. Monday might be potato dumplings stuffed with meat; Tuesday, heart and liver served with bread crumb dumplings; Wednesday, lasagna; Thursday, deep-fried, breaded beef; and Friday, beans and sausage. Otherwise, choices include hot and cold sandwiches, chili con carne, a pasta or two, the usual Viennese dishes of pork, breaded cutlets, goulash, and four desserts.

HOURS
Mon–Sat 11 A.M.–1 A.M., Sun 11 A.M.–midnight, continuous service

RESERVATIONS
Only for large groups

CREDIT CARDS
Not accepted

À LA CARTE
Sandwiches 40–65AS; full-course meals 125–200AS

FIXED-PRICE MENU
Lunch Mon–Fri (until 3 P.M.), 60AS, garnished main course

SERVICE
Service included

ENGLISH
Yes, and menu in English

(56) SPATZENNEST
A-1070, St. Ulrichsplatz 1

A memorable meal at the popular Spatzennest (which means "sparrow's nest") centers on time-honored Viennese specialties. The restaurant is always filled with smart locals who know good food when they taste it and value when they find it. During the winter, everyone crowds into the little rooms, filling the wall hooks with their heavy coats. In the summer, diners stretch out onto the outdoor terrace and enjoy the sun.

The menu is seasonal, and in winter begins with a light, yet warming liver dumpling soup, deep-fried mushrooms, or a beef-based salad. Game always has a starring role at this time of year, and the roast hare in cream sauce is a delicious example. This is also the place to try roast deer with pepper sauce or the comforting *Zwiebelroastbraten,* braised beef with onions.

Chocolate lovers will be happy with one of the best *Mohr im Hemd* served in Vienna—a chocolate bundt-style cake served with chocolate sauce and whipped cream just to gild the lily. Another delicious dessert option at least one of you must order is the *Kaiserschmarren,* or

TELEPHONE
526 16 59

U-BAHN
2, 3, Volkstheater

OPEN
Sun–Thur

CLOSED
Fri–Sat; first 3 weeks in August

HOURS
10 A.M.–midnight, continuous service

RESERVATIONS
Essential

CREDIT CARDS
MC, V

À LA CARTE
190–240AS

FIXED-PRICE MENU
None

SERVICE
Service included

ENGLISH
Yes, and menu in English

Emperor's trifle, a sweet omelette served with a side dish of stewed plums.

Cafés

(57) CAFÉ JELINEK
A-1060, Otto Bauer Gasse 5

TELEPHONE
597 41 13

U-BAHN
3, Neubaugasse

OPEN
Mon–Fri

CLOSED
Sat–Sun, holidays

HOURS
8 A.M.–8 P.M., fixed-price lunch
12:15–2 P.M.

RESERVATIONS
Not necessary

CREDIT CARDS
Not accepted

À LA CARTE
Coffee from 38AS, pastries from
50AS, breakfast 40–80AS,
lunch 100–150AS

FIXED-PRICE MENU
Lunch, 70–90AS, one course

SERVICE
No service charged or expected

ENGLISH
Sometimes (if their daughter is
there)

The Café Jelinek has been on this corner near the popular Mariahilferstrasse shopping street since 1919, and it is the type of place you would adopt as your regular coffeehouse if you lived nearby. For the past ten or more years, Günter Knopp and his wife have been welcoming their dedicated guests, who have come to appreciate Günter's homemade pastries. Try a piece of his *Guglhupf*—a buttery marble cake that goes perfectly with hot chocolate topped with cinnamon and whipped cream on a cold, wintery day. If you are here around noon, they also serve delicious lunches.

The inside of the café has a well-worn, cozy feeling. Downstairs has comfortable chairs placed around bare, marble-topped tables, and upstairs the setting becomes a bit more formal with lace tablecloths. The old brass stove stands proudly by the blanket-draped entry, and the assorted posters and wallpaper age gracefully—little has changed in the café over the years, and probably never will. Let's hope not!

Near the Naschmarkt

Naschmarkt is the big, sprawling outdoor food market right in the center of Vienna. If you love food, you must allow at least an hour or so to wander through it. Saturday morning, when the flea market is going on at the back end, is the most crowded. There are no undiscovered bargains at the flea market, but if you look hard enough, you are bound to find something of interest.

RESTAURANTS

Restaurants

(58) HEINDL & CO.
A-1040, Naschmarkt 130–138

While you are at the Naschmarkt, plan on having your breakfast or lunch at Heindl & Co., long known for dishing out some of the best sweet and savory pancakes in Vienna. You eat your meal seated at a U-shaped bar, where you can watch the cook dip into the big bowl of pancake batter as he makes each order.

You can be virtuous and have yours with cheese and vegetables, or have the delicious duet of *Palatschinken* covered in chocolate sauce and whipped cream, or the one with vanilla pudding topped with rum-soaked fruit and whipped cream.

TELEPHONE
587 87 44

U-BAHN
1, 2, 4, Karlsplatz, exit Session

OPEN
Mon–Sat

CLOSED
Sun, holidays

HOURS
Mon–Fri 6 A.M.–6 P.M., Sat 6 A.M.–2 P.M., continuous service

RESERVATIONS
Not necessary

CREDIT CARDS
Not accepted

À LA CARTE
65–100AS

FIXED-PRICE MENU
None

SERVICE
No service charged or expected

ENGLISH
No, but menu in English

(59) MENSA
A-1040, Wiedner Hauptstrasse 8–19 (first floor of Technische Universität, Turm B)

TELEPHONE
216 06 68

U-BAHN
1, 2, 4, Karlsplatz

OPEN
Mon–Fri lunch only

CLOSED
Sat–Sun, holidays

HOURS
11 A.M.–2:30 P.M.

RESERVATIONS
Not accepted

CREDIT CARDS
Not accepted

À LA CARTE
Students, 40–50AS; non-students, 45–80AS

FIXED-PRICE MENU
None

SERVICE
No service charged or expected

ENGLISH
Yes

MISCELLANEOUS
Nonsmoking section

Mensa, the student cafeteria on the first floor of the Technical University of Vienna, serves huge lunchtime meals for both students (with I.D.) and nonstudents. There is also a grill restaurant open the same hours, where one-plate meals go for 50 to 65AS. At the cafeteria you can select as much or as little as you like, starting with a salad bar. Beer, wine, and even carrot juice are available, and there is a nonsmoking section where you can sit. If you piled everything in sight on your tray, you couldn't spend 100AS.

Wiener Heurigen
(Vienna Wine Taverns)

Heurige is the Viennese word both for the wine from the last grape harvest and for the establishment where it is served (the plural is *Heurigen*). It is said that a stay in Vienna without visiting a *Heurige* would be missing a chance to get to know "the heart of the Viennese and their well-known *Gemütlichkeit* [sociability]."

These authentic wine-growing districts are in the Vienna woods in the outskirts of the city proper, but they are still considered part of greater Vienna. Fortunately, most of them have retained their old village atmosphere, with narrow winding streets and stone walls surrounding the houses and taverns. According to laws set by the Emperor Josef II in 1784, and still in force, real *Heurigen* are only allowed to be open three hundred days in one year and may only sell food and wine produced on the premises. If the *Heurige* is *ausg'stect* (open), a sprig of pine will be hanging over the entrance. It should be noted that many of the *Heurigen* have skirted this law by obtaining restaurant licenses enabling them to be open almost continuously. Most *Heurigen* open late in the afternoon, and the more touristy ones offer some sort of live music. Food is usually self-service buffet style, and it is not the draw—wine drinking is. The wine served will be *Heuriger* (wine from the most recent vintage) or *Alter* (the previous year's vintage), and it will be brought to your table, but you are expected to get your food yourself from the buffet spread.

The list of *Heurigen* in *Cheap Eats* is by no means definitive. It is only meant to be a starting place, since half the fun of going to these picturesque places is to wander through the villages and discover the ones that appeal to you. In the winter, you will be joined mostly by the Viennese, but in the summer, especially in Grinzing, watch out, as many of the taverns are totally overrun by tour bus groups. Depending on which village you select, the trip from Vienna by public transportation should take from thirty minutes to one hour.

WIENER HEURIGEN

NOTE: *Wiener Heurigen* do not appear on the Vienna city map.

Grinzing

Grinzing is the best-known wine district and certainly the most tourist-oriented. Here you will find all the different kinds of *Heuriger,* from the simple to the most smaltzy. This is where the composer Ludwig van Beethoven had one of his many homes, and where he sought inspiration on his long walks over glasses of new wine. Getting to Grinzing is easy. From the Schottentor stop of U-Bahn line 2, take tram No. 38 to the end of the line. To avoid the worst on this wine tourist trail, keep walking up Cobenzlgasse to No. 15, Altes Presshaus, the oldest wine tavern in Grinzing, with its original wine cellar still in tact.

ALTES PRESSHAUS
A-1190, Coblenzlgasse 15

TELEPHONE: 32 23 93

U-BAHN: 2, Schottentor, then tram No. 38 to end of the line

OPEN: Daily

CLOSED: Jan, Feb

HOURS: 4 P.M.–midnight

RESERVATIONS: On weekends in the summer

CREDIT CARDS: AE, MC, V

À LA CARTE: 165–300AS

FIXED-PRICE MENU: None

SERVICE: No service charged or expected

ENGLISH: Yes

Heiligenstadt

The next most popular wine producing villages are Heiligenstadt and Nussdorf. In Heiligenstadt, stop in at Mayer am Pfarrplatz, the house where Beethoven composed part of his Ninth Symphony. Today, the Mayer family offers a buffet, prize-winning wines, and a romantic garden.

MAYER AM PFARRPLATZ
A-1190, Pfarrplatz 2

TELEPHONE: 37 12 87

U-BAHN: 4, Heiligenstadt, then bus No. 38A

OPEN: Daily

CLOSED: Dec 22–Jan 10

HOURS: Mon–Sat 4 P.M.–midnight, Sun 11 A.M.–midnight

RESERVATIONS: Suggested on the weekends

CREDIT CARDS: AE, DC, MC, V

À LA CARTE: 180–250AS

FIXED-PRICE MENU: None

SERVICE: No service charged or expected

ENGLISH: Yes

Nussdorf

In Nussdorf, the Kierlinger has been in the same family since 1787. Their wine speciality is a Riesling-Traminer. Also in Nussdorf is Schubel-Auer, which has several small, intimate rooms that attract local crowds on the weekends.

KIERLINGER
A-1190, Kahlenberger Strasse 20

TELEPHONE: 37 22 64

U-BAHN: 4, Heiligenstadt, then Tram D to end of the line

OPEN: Daily

CLOSED: Easter, last 2 weeks in Aug and Oct

HOURS: 3:30 P.M.–midnight

RESERVATIONS: Not necessary

CREDIT CARDS: Not accepted

À LA CARTE: 160–200AS

FIXED-PRICE MENU: None

SERVICE: No service charged or expected

ENGLISH: Yes

SCHUBEL-AUER
A-1190, Kahlenberger Strasse 22

TELEPHONE: 37 22 22

U-BAHN: 4, Heiligenstadt, then Tram D to end of the line

OPEN: Mon–Sat

CLOSED: Sun; Jan

HOURS: 4 P.M.–midnight

RESERVATIONS: Suggested on Fri and Sat

CREDIT CARDS: Not accepted

À LA CARTE: 90–165AS

FIXED-PRICE MENU: None

SERVICE: No service charged or expected

ENGLISH: Limited

Stammersdorf

Stammersdorf is the largest wine growing area and one that is popular with the Viennese. If you go here, try Wieninger; its wines are considered some of the best in Austria.

WIENINGER
Stammersdorfer Strasse 78

TELEPHONE: 292 41 06

U-BAHN: 2, 4, Schottenring, then Tram No. 31 to end of the line

OPEN: Wed–Sun

CLOSED: Mon–Tues; mid-Dec–March

HOURS: Wed–Fri 3 P.M.–midnight, Sat 2 P.M.–midnight, Sun 1 P.M.–midnight

RESERVATIONS: Suggested on weekends and holidays

CREDIT CARDS: Not accepted

À LA CARTE: 100–175AS

FIXED-PRICE MENU: None

SERVICE: No service charged or expected

ENGLISH: Yes

Glossary of Helpful Phrases and Menu Terms

Though Austrians speak German with an accent, and the Viennese have their own dialect, most use standard German when speaking to a foreigner. No one will expect a visitor to Vienna to know all the complexities of the German language, and most people you will encounter will have some knowledge of English. However, if you can learn a few phrases and words, your efforts will be appreciated.

General Phrases

Do you speak English?	*Sprechen Sie Englisch?*
I do not speak German	*Ich spreche kein Deutsch*
I understand	*Ich verstehe*
I do not understand	*Ich verstehe nicht*
yes/no	*ja/nein*
good day	*Grüss Gott, Guten Tag*
good morning	*Guten Morgen*
good evening	*Guten Abend*
good night	*Gute Nacht*
good-bye	*Auf Wiedersehen*
please/you are welcome	*bitte (schön)*
thank you/very much	*danke/danke schön, vielen Dank*
excuse me	*Entschuldigen Sie*
Mr./Mrs./Miss	*Herr/Frau/Fräulein*
May I?	*Darf ich?*
big/small	*gross/klein*
more/less	*mehr/weniger*
good/bad	*gut/schlecht*
open	*geöffnet, offen, auf*
closed	*geschlossen, zu*

Numbers and Letters

0	*null*
1	*eins*
2	*zwei*
3	*drei*
4	*vier*
5	*fünf*
6	*sechs*
7	*sieben*
8	*acht*
9	*neun*

10	*zehn*
11	*elf*
12	*zwölf*
13	*dreizehn*
14	*vierzehn*
15	*fünfzehn*
16	*sechzehn*
17	*siebzehn*
18	*achtzehn*
19	*neunzehn*
20	*zwanzig*
21	*ein-und-zwanzig*
22	*zwei-und-zwanzig*
30	*dreissig*
40	*vierzig*
50	*fünfzig*
60	*sechzig*
70	*siebzig*
80	*achtzig*
90	*neunzig*
100	*hundert*
1,000	*tausend*
ss (double "s")	*ß (esszed)*

Days of the Week

Monday	*Montag*
Tuesday	*Dienstag*
Wednesday	*Mittwoch*
Thursday	*Donnerstag*
Friday	*Freitag*
Saturday	*Samstag*
Sunday	*Sonntag*
today	*heute*
yesterday	*gestern*
tomorrow	*morgen*
the day before yesterday	*vorgestern*
the day after tomorrow	*übermorgen*
week	*Woche*

Eating Out

Bon appetit!/Cheers!	*Guten Appetit!/Prost!*
The menu, please	*die Speisekarte bitte*
The bill, please	*die Rechnung bitte*
waiter/waitress	*Herr Ober/Fräulein*
Do you have	*Haben Sie*
set menu	*ein Tagesgedeck/Gedeck*

breakfast	*Frühstück*
lunch	*Mittagessen*
dinner	*Abendessen*
cup	*Tasse*
fork	*Gabel*
glass	*Glas*
knife	*Messer*
napkin	*Serviette*
plate	*Teller*
spoon	*Löffel*

Basic Menu Terms

belegtes Brot	open-face sandwiches
Beilagen	extras: vegetables, salads, and so on
Butter	butter
Getränke inbegriffen	drink included
Hauptgerichte	main courses
kalte Speisen	cold main courses
kalte Vorgerichte	cold first courses or appetizers
Käse	cheese
kleine Gerichte	small courses, hot or cold
Marmelade	jam
Pfeffer	pepper
Salz	salt
Spezialitäten	specialties of the house
Tagesmenü	dish of the day
Tellergerichte	hot or cold one-plate meals
warme Vorgerichte	hot first courses or appetizers
Vorspeisen	appetizers
Zucker	sugar
Zuschlag	extra charge

Methods of Preparation

blau	boiled in salt and vinegar
blutig	rare
gebraten	baked, roasted
gebacken	fried
gedämpft	steamed
gedünstet	braised
gegrillit	grilled
gekocht	boiled
gepökelt	cured
geschwenkt	sautéed
geschmort	stewed
gut durchgebraten	well-done
Mittel	medium

paniert	breaded
pochiert	poached
roh	raw
fertige speisen	ready cooked

Meat (*Fleisch*)

Bauernschmaus	pork and ham platter
Hammel	mutton
Kalb	veal
Kitz	goat
Kuttelfleck	tripe
Lamm	lamb
Leber	liver
Nieren	kidneys
Rind	beef
Schinken	ham
Schinkenfleckerln	ham with noodles
Schwein	pork
Speck	bacon
Tafelspitz	boiled beef
Wiener Schnitzel	breaded veal
Wurst	sausage

Game (*Wild*)

Hase	hare
Hirsch	deer
Kaninchen	rabbit
Reh	venison

Poultry (*Geflügel*)

Backhendl	chicken fried in bread crumbs
Ente	duck
Fasan	pheasant
Gans	goose
Huhn	chicken
Puter	turkey
Taube	pigeon

Fish (*Fisch*)

Aal	eel
Austern	oysters
Flunder	flounder
Forelle	trout
Garnelen	prawns
Heilbutt	halibut

Hummer	lobster
Kabeljau	cod
Karpfen	carp
Krebs	crab, crayfish
Lachs	salmon
Languste	spiny lobster, crawfish
Matjes	herring
Muscheln	mussels
Rotbarsch	red sea bass
Seezunge	sole
Tintenfisch	cuttlefish
Thunfisch	tuna

Soups (*Suppen*)

Griessnockerlsuppe	semolina dumpling soup
Gulaschsuppe	goulash soup
Hühnersuppe	chicken soup
Kartoffelsuppe	potato soup
Knoblauchsuppe	garlic soup
Leberknödelsuppe	liver dumpling soup
Ochsenschwanzsuppe	oxtail soup

Eggs (*Eier*)

Eierspeisen	egg dishes
Ei mit Speck	bacon and eggs
Einlauf	with egg in it
Gekochtes Ei	boiled eggs
Rühreier	scrambled eggs
Spiegelei	fried eggs

Side Dishes (*Beilagen*)

Nudel	noodles
Kartoffelsalat	potato salad, hot or cold
Krapfen/Kucherl	fritters
Salat	salad
Spätzle	short, bumpy egg noodles
Nockerln	dumplings

Vegetables (*Gemüse*)

Aubergine	eggplant
Bohnen	beans
Blumenkohl	cauliflower
Champignons	small mushrooms
Erbsen	peas
Gurke	cucumber
Karotten	carrots

Kartoffel	potato
Knoblauch	garlic
Kraut	herb, vegetable, cabbage
Lattich	lettuce
Lauch	leek
Mais/Maiskolben	corn/on the cob
Mischgemüse	mixed vegetables
Paprika	pepper
Rote Beete	red beet
Rotkohl (Kraut)	red cabbage
Sellerie	celery
Spargel	asparagus
Zwiebeln	onions

Fruit (*Obst*)

Ananas	pineapple
Apfel	apple
Apfelsine	orange
Aprikose	apricot
Brombeere	blackberry
Erdberre	strawberry
Heidelbeere	blueberry
Kirsche	cherry
Pamplemuse	grapefruit
Rosine	raisin

Desserts (*Nachspeisen*)

Nachspeise/Nachtisch	dessert/sweet
Apfelstrudel	thin layers of dough with apples
Buchtelm	sweet dumplings
Eiskreme	ice cream
Gebäck	pastry
Guglhupf	sponge cake
Käsekuchen	cheesecake
Königskucken	rum-flavored loaf cake with almonds, raisins, and currants
Kuchen	cake, tart, or pastry
Lenkucken	gingerbread
Linzertorte	jam tart with almond-flavored pastry
Mohr in Hemd	chocolate pudding with ice cream
Moohrenkopf	"Moor's Head," a dome-shaped individual white cake filled with custard or whipped cream and covered with hardened chocolate
Palatschinken	sweet filled pancakes
Sachertorte	rich chocolate layer cake with jam
Sahne	cream, plain or whipped

Salzburger Nockerl	sweet dough dumplings, poached in milk, served with hot vanilla sauce
Schlagobers	whipped cream
Stollen	a dense cake with raisins, almonds, nuts, and candied lemon peel
Topfenstrudel	a creamed cottage cheese strudel

Drinks (*Getränke*)

Bier/dunkles/helles	beer/dark/light
Fruchtsaft	fruit juice
Glüwein	mulled wine
Kaffee/braun/schwarz	coffee/with milk, cream/black
koffeinfrei, Hag	decaffeinated
Milch	milk
Tee/Zitronentee	tea/with lemon
Wasser/Mineralwasser	water/mineral water
Wein/rot/weiss/schaum	wine/red/white/sparkling

BUDAPEST

Hungarian food bears the influence of centuries of foreign occupation, most notably by the Turks, who dominated Hungary for 150 years. Coffee, melons, tropical fruits, nuts, spices, and many seasonings were all introduced by conquering foes. Paprika invaded the country with the Turkish in the fifteenth century, and at first it was considered a spice used by peasants who could not afford more expensive imported spices. Gradually its use grew, and today no Hungarian kitchen would be without a liberal supply. Where Westerners use it as a colorful garnish, the Hungarian cook uses it as an indispensable ingredient to give dishes a piquant flavor and aroma—and it has become the defining ingredient of the national cuisine. Sour cream is almost as widely used. It is not really sour, but it looks like whipped cream and adds tang to meats, soups, vegetables, and desserts.

There are over five thousand restaurants (six hundred with gypsy violinists) in Budapest alone, and they range from *étkezdék*—those simple homespun lunchrooms with a few shared tables and five or six daily changing main courses—to formal restaurants with beautifully set tables. The collapse of Communism and the rise of capitalism has brought fast-food outlets such as McDonald's, Burger King, and Kentucky Fried Chicken to almost every neighborhood. It has also created a huge influx of tourist interest in Budapest and, as a result, encouraged restaurant owners to improve quality, demand a more professional attitude from their staff, and cater to a more international audience. Sometimes it works. Other times it fails miserably, and both can happen in the same week at the same restaurant.

Cheap Eating in Budapest is very easy to do. In fact, most meals cost much less than in other European capitals. While Hungarian cuisine is easy on the budget and plentiful on the plate, it is ruinous to most waistlines. As in Prague, grease, fat, sugar, starch, and cream—all but the last fried—are considered the five basic food groups, and it is no wonder that Hungarians suffer more gout and heart disease than any other population in central Europe. Many think incorrectly that the food is spicy. After all, isn't it all covered with paprika? Some of it is, yes, but most dishes are bland, heavy, and centered around rich meat, wild game, and goose liver with cream gravies and garnishes of potatoes and sauerkraut. The most popular preparations are larded, breaded, and fried—with the exception of meat-filled cabbage rolls, chicken in paprika-flavored sour cream, and sturdy meat stews that simmer for days and stick to your ribs for weeks. Desserts are also sinfully rich, and the highlights are sponge cake spiked with rum and covered with cream and chocolate sauce (*somlói galuska*), fruit wrapped in dumplings dressed in

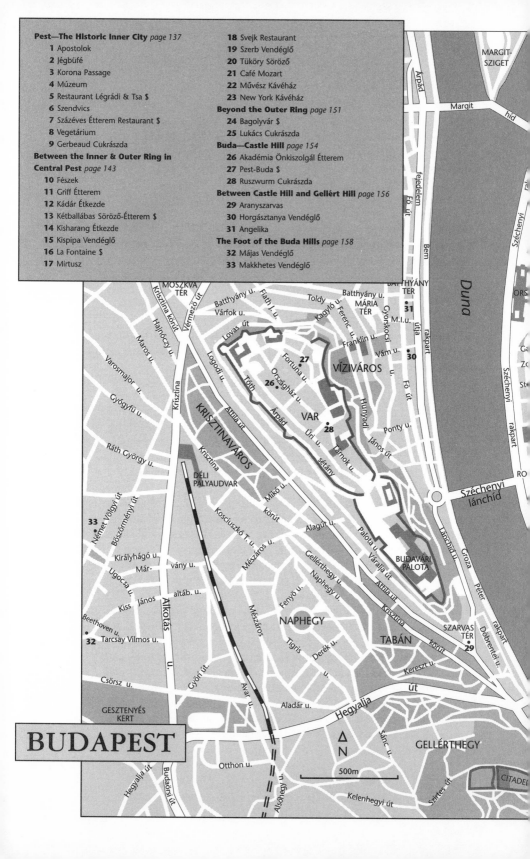

BUDAPEST

chocolate sauce and whipped cream (*palacsinta*), and strudels (*rétes*) filled with cream, cherries, apples, or poppyseeds.

Coffee is one of the most enduring legacies of the Ottoman-Turkish empire. At the turn of the century, more than five hundred coffeehouses catered to Budapest residents, and they were a vibrant force in the culture of the city. These cafés were both elegant and intimate. Many provided their regular customers with pens, ink, paper, and newspapers, and they even sent couriers on errands for them, to take shoes to be polished or to buy tobacco. People came early and stayed late, playing cards, billiards, and chess; they conducted business and discussed politics, made friends, and wrote plays and novels. Jeno Heltai, a noted Hungarian playwright, has said, "Cafés forced people to behave more politely and have better manners. They educated and displined people. They informed, enlightened, and cultivated people." Thanks to the worldwide depression in the 1930s, the subsequent hardships encountered during World War II, and finally, Communist rule, the grand coffeehouses—and the culture surrounding them—have almost all disappeared. The few that remain are mere shadows of their glorious past.

For ease and convenience, the Cheap Eat listings in Budapest are divided by the Danube River: first are those in Pest (the flat, commercial side of the city), and then those in Buda (the hilly, more residential side). I wish you *jó étvágyat!*

Cheap Eating Tips in Budapest

1. Leave gourmet expectations and most dietary concerns at the Hungarian border.

2. Eating or drinking while standing at the bar of a coffeehouse or pastry shop is not customary. You are expected to sit at a table and be served.

3. Cheap Eating is possible in most restaurants at any time of day, but to take advantage of many fixed-price menus and the blue-plate specials, go for lunch.

4. Long menus should be cause for skepticism. Smart Cheap Eaters know that most kitchens can't juggle such a wide array of offerings with any degree of consistency, which means that many of these foods live long lives in the freezer.

5. As a consequence, for the freshest dishes, order the daily specials or the specialties of the house.

6. Dining in Budapest usually requires patience, and sometimes plenty of it. Service varies from polite and acceptable to slow, rude, and almost nonexistent.

7. When reserving a table, ask your hotel to make the booking. This adds a little clout on your behalf and should help to cut back on the rampant overcharging that unfortunately occurs in some restaurants.

8. Sometimes, menus handed to women diners and those printed in English bear no prices. Insist on a menu that lists the prices, and if the restaurant refuses, get up and leave.

9. Always add up the bill yourself to be sure it is correct. When you are ready to pay, and if the tip is extra, include it in the total and tell the waiter how much you are paying, including the tip. (For more on paying the bill and avoiding rip-offs, see Paying the Bill and Tipping, page 134.)

10. Finally, here is how to deal with gypsy violinists:

    a: Tip heavily and they will play at your table all night.

    b: Ignore them and they will play anyway, usually as close to your face and ears as possible.

    c: Insult them with a meager tip but act very generous when handing it over, and they will soon move on to greener pastures.

General Information about Cheap Eating in Budapest

A real Hungarian can handle his paprika well.
—Hungarian saying

Where to Eat

Despite great improvement in the city's number and quality of restaurants in recent years, no one could honestly describe Budapest as a gourmet mecca. On the other hand, the city has a reputation for reasonable prices, and many restaurants are open nonstop, which is a boon for many visitors.

The word for restaurant—*étterem*—can be applied to any place that serves food, from the most expensive to the little neighborhood spot with only two or three tables. At midday, look for *étkezde*, cheap diners open only for lunch. A self-service cafeteria—*önkiszolgáló*—is also popular for a Cheap Eat lunch with little pretense. The Cheapest Eat in Budapest is a *kolbász* (sausage) sold in a butcher shop. Along with your *kolbász*, you can order knockwurst, smoked ham, or blood sausage. Everything is sold by weight; bread, mustard, and pickles are extra. A *vendéglő* is a small restaurant, open for lunch and dinner. For a coffee and sweet, go to a *cukrászda* or *kávéház*, and for a quick, stand-up meal, grab a bite at a *bufé*.

What to Eat

For Hungarians, the spirit in which a dish is cooked is almost as important as the ingredients and the measurements. But for most foreigners, Hungarian food means "goulash." The dish is usually made with chicken or beef, plentifully laden with Hungary's favorite condiment, sweet or hot paprika. Other Hungarian favorites include the famous *Balaton fogás*, a variety of lake fish, and red bacon, once considered a peasant dish, which is made by dipping fatty bacon pieces into paprika and leaving them to marinate until they become red. Noodles with melted butter and poppyseeds are also popular.

The main meal is usually lunch, and that is when food will be at its freshest, especially in smaller places where many unsold lunch dishes rest on the back burner until being rewarmed for the dinner trade. Daily specials are made in limited amounts, and when they're gone, they're gone. The Hungarian menu *(étlap)* begins with appetizers *(előételek)* of goose liver and breaded, deep-fried mushrooms or cauliflower. Main courses *(főételek)* lean heavily on stewed meats, wild game, and chicken with sour cream. Fresh pike-perch from Lake Balaton is delicious, and so are the stuffed cabbage rolls. Vegetables are not a highlight in most restaurants, except for the ubiquitous potato.

Hungarians know no shame when it comes to desserts. Budapest is loaded with pastry shops and cafés serving strudels—which are made with cream, cherries, apples, cheese, nuts, jam, or poppyseeds and wrapped in layers of flaky filo dough. The national dessert is considered by many to be *dobos torta,* a multilayered confection of chocolate and caramel, and many other decadent pastries are lavishly layered with this same configuration of delights: vanilla, chocolate, caramel, fruits, cream fillings, and mounds of whipped cream on top. On Sunday afternoon you will see entire families out for an afternoon devoted to unabashedly satisfying their sweet tooth.

What to Drink

The Slovaks all drink brandy,
The Germans all drink beer,
The Hungarians drink wine only,
The very best, my dear.
—*Hungarian folk song*

There are twenty distinct wine-growing regions in Hungary, each with its own special soil and climate, creating a great variety of Hungarian wines. White wines from the Balaton and Szekszard regions are dry and fruity. For red, some of the best come from Villany. Tokay is the famous dessert wine, and Bull's Blood is a strong red blend. Refined wine drinkers go to a wine bar. Others frequent *borozó,* stand-up wine bars that are often full at 9 A.M. These establishments provide food only to keep the regulars from falling on their faces, and it usually consists of bread and pork drippings topped with paprika and onions.

If you are insistent on drinking Hungarian beer—which is generally not up to the standards set by Prague and Budapest—the cheapest and most popular brew is Aranyaszok, a draught beer made by the Kőbányai Brewery in Pest. Important: For reasons that are not clear to me, clinking beer mugs is *never* done. Hungarian spirits are heavy on the aromatics—herbs, fruit, and spices—which are considered healthy counterattacks to the robust cuisine. The best known is Unicum, a bitter, twenty-three-herb concoction thought by many to be a tonic for an overindulgent meal. Fruit brandies are also popular tonics, especially *barackpálinka,* an apricot brandy, which serves as a digestive aid or a fast wake-up call in the morning.

Coffeehouses in Budapest began with the Turks and were in full-flower long before they became popular in Vienna. Their golden age has long since passed, but there are still a few today where lingering over a coffee and a slice of rich pastry for hours remains a way of life. All the same coffees served in Vienna are served here (see page 74 for a full description), table sharing is acceptable, and you can occupy your seat for as long as you like.

Reservations

Reservations are important, especially in the more expensive restaurants. Unless your Hungarian is fluent, have your hotel book your table. That way the restaurant will have to answer to the hotel and risk the loss of future business if you were not treated correctly. This applies especially to the rampant bill padding.

Paying the Bill and Tipping

Much of the advice for paying your bill in Prague pertains to Budapest. You will not be presented with your bill until you ask for it. Signal someone that you are ready to pay, and the bill-collecting person will come to your table to tally up your total, often asking what you have had. Look at the bill very carefully because mistakes are unfortunately the rule, not the exception. Feel free to question any suspicious amounts. When you are satisfied that everything is correct, state the amount you are paying including the tip and hand all of the money to the person— don't leave the tip on the table. If paying by credit card, include the tip on the card, draw lines through all other blank spaces, and write out the total figure you are paying, such as, four hundred and fifty forints.

As in Prague, some restaurants include a service charge with your bill (usually 10 to 15 percent), and remember that this *is* the tip. If the service is included, you do not have to tip anything else unless you have had exceptional service. Other places do not include a service charge but still expect a tip (usually 10 to 15 percent), and others do not charge for nor expect a tip. Each listing in *Cheap Eats in Budapest* notes what to expect, as follows: service included; service discretionary; or no service charged or expected.

Holidays

Shops, museums, banks, and some restaurants are closed on holidays. For the week from Christmas to New Year's, Budapest almost completely shuts down (including all forms of public transportation) beginning at noon on December 24. Transportation gets back into swing by December 27, but the city does not return to full speed until after January 1.

January 1	New Year's Day
March 15	National Holiday
Easter Sunday	Dates vary
Easter Monday	Dates vary
May 1	Labor Day
6th Monday after Easter	Whit Monday
August 20	St. Stephen's Day
October 23	Remembrance Day
December 25/26	Christmas

Finding an Address

Unless you've been to Budapest before, finding an address in the city can be a very frustrating exercise guaranteed to test your patience and perseverance.

Budapest is divided into twenty-three districts, or zones, called *kerület*, or *ker* for short. All Budapest addresses are preceded by a Roman numeral that indicates the *kerület*. Because many streets in different parts of the city bear the same name, it is vital to know what *kerület* the address is in. For example, "V. Vaci *utca* 8" means that the address is in the fifth *kerület*. If there is no Roman numeral before the address, you can still tell the *kerület* from the postal code, since the middle two digits represent the *kerület*. For example, "Vaci *utca* 8, 1053" means it is in the fifth *kerület*.

Once you know the *kerület*, you have to know what type of street you are looking for. The most common mistake is with *utca*, which means street. In addresses, it is almost always abbreviated as "u.," and it should not be confused with *út*, which is a wide street or avenue. The definitions below should help you find your way.

fasor	alley
híd	bridge
körút (krt.)	boulevard, ring road
körtér	circle
köz	lane
liget	park
part	riverbank
pályaudvar (pu.)	railway/metro station
rakpart	embankment
sétány	walk
sziget	island
sor	row
tér	square
tere	square of
udvar	arcade, passageway
utca (u.)	street
út	wide road or avenue
útja	road of

Transportation

The public transportation system in Budapest is easy to use. The most important point to remember is that every time you transfer from one bus to another or from one underground direction to another, you *must* use another ticket. There are only three metro lines, and they are listed in text (along with the nearest metro stop) as follows: M1 (yellow line), M2 (red line), and M3 (blue line).

Taxis, however, can be a nightmare, and some Budapest taxi drivers are rightfully dubbed *hyenas*. It is a fact that many are dishonest and unscrupulous and regard tourists as fair game. For these mean-spirited drivers, there is no limit to what they will do to outfox, outwit, outsmart, and ultimately cheat you.

The best way to avoid being cheated is to call one of the taxi companies listed below, or to insist that the hotel receptionist call one for you. Avoid any private taxi—those lined up in front of your hotel, the railway station, the airport, and at tourist sites. When you reserve, ask what the general price should be to your destination, and when you get in the taxi, be sure the meter is turned on. The rates are convoluted at best—they vary according to the time of day and the zones traveled through—but you have a right to know ahead of time what you can expect to be charged. A small tip is appreciated, but not required.

Buda Taxi:	120-0200
City Taxi:	211-1111, dispatchers usually speak English
Főtaxi:	222-2222

Important Telephone Notice

The telephone system in Hungary is being privatized. This means that although the telephone numbers for the listings in this section were correct at press time, they may have changed by your arrival. If you are calling from the United States and you dial a number that's no longer working, dial 00 and ask for international directory assistance. The operator will connect you with an English-speaking operator in Budapest. If you are calling from Budapest, ask your hotel desk clerk to assist you. He or she may have access to the most up-to-date information.

Restaurants in Budapest by Area

PEST

Central Pest is the part of the city lying between the River Danube and the boulevards forming the Outer Ring, which are named after former Hungarian monarchs: Ferenc körút, József körút, Erzsébet körút, Teréz körút, and Szent István körút. The Outer Ring begins on the Pest side of the Petőfi híd (bridge) in the southern part of the city and ends at the Margit híd in the north.

Restaurants and coffeehouses on the Pest side of the Danube are grouped according to location: The Historic Inner City, Between the Inner and Outer Rings of Central Pest, and Beyond the Outer Ring.

The Historic Inner City

The Historic Inner City of Pest starts at Szabadság híd (Freedom Bridge) and winds through Vámház körút, Múzeum körút, Károly körút, Bajcsy-Zsilinszky út, and Jozsef Attila utca. It ends at the Széchenyi lánchíd (The Chain Bridge). This is an area of many luxury hotels, some of the best shopping, and many historic buildings.

RESTAURANTS

CAFÉS AND PASTRY SHOPS

A dollar sign ($) indicates a Big Splurge.

Restaurants

(1) APOSTOLOK
V. Kígyó u. 4–6

TELEPHONE
267-0290

METRO
M3, Ferenciek tere

OPEN
Daily

CLOSED
Never

HOURS
Noon–midnight, continuous
service

RESERVATIONS
Suggested for lunch, essential
for dinner

CREDIT CARDS
AE, DC, MC, V

À LA CARTE
2,200–3,000Ft

FIXED-PRICE MENU
None

SERVICE
Service discretionary

ENGLISH
Yes, and menu in English

The interior of Apostolok, which dates back to 1913, is one of the most impressive in Budapest. A beautiful tiled-floor entry leads along a wood-paneled corridor lined with old church pews. The larger of the restaurant's two rooms displays a fire enamel mosaic of the twelve apostles; the smaller is dominated by a lead-glass window copied from *The Offering of the Crown to the Blessed Virgin,* the original of which is in the St. Stephen Basilica of Budapest. The booth-style seating resembling church pews adds to the overall atmosphere.

The chefs in the open kitchen turn out an appealing array of Hungarian and international dishes. For appetizers, I suggest skipping the soups and trying the homemade goose liver on toast or the deep-fried cheese wrapped with ham and served with baked apple slices. If you don't have the cold goose liver to start, try it breaded and fried and served with a green salad as your main course. Other choices are grilled pork chops with dumplings and mushroom sauce, filet mignon with herb butter, or dilled turkey and mushrooms accompanied with rice and corn. Salads are above average, ranging from a selection of the chef's own pickles to white cabbage tossed in vinegar dressing. The best dessert is either the *somlói galuska*—rum-custard sponge cake with chocolate sauce and whipped cream—or the *Gundel palacsinta*—sweet crêpes filled with ground nuts, rum, and sugar and covered with chocolate sauce.

(2) JÉGBÜFÉ
V. Ferenciek tere 10

TELEPHONE
267-3275

METRO
M3, Ferenciek tere

OPEN
Daily

CLOSED
Christmas

HOURS
7 A.M.–9 P.M., continuous service

RESERVATIONS
Not accepted

CREDIT CARDS
AE

For a coffee or a snack, you will seldom have a Cheaper Eat anywhere on this planet than at Jégbüfé, a stand-up coffee, pastry, and ice cream shop on Ferenciek tere. Ice cream is well under a dollar for a triple-scoop cone, and fancy cake slices and other pastries are priced at the same give-away level. An espresso coffee costs around 30¢, a cappuccino about 50¢, and a hot chocolate a whopping 65¢ or 70¢. Here is the drill: Look around, decide what you want, pay at one of the two cash registers, and then go back with your paid receipt to the counter, where you will be handed your food and drink. Then you find a place to stand and eat along the counters facing the window. It is all easy, quick, and oh, so cheap.

À LA CARTE
100–200Ft
FIXED-PRICE MENU
None
SERVICE
No service charged or expected
ENGLISH
Limited, but it won't matter

(3) KORONA PASSAGE
V. Kecskeméti u. 14

Lots of possibilities, from light snacks to full meals, exist at the Korona Passage, a restaurant specializing in crêpes in the Korona Hotel. The room has an open, airy feeling, with a pitched glass roof, green trees and plants, and a front-facing wall of windows. Young girls in green-and-white striped uniforms take your sweet or savory crêpe orders and prepare them while you watch. The fillings are the usual: ham, cheese, mushroom, vegetable, tomato, and egg, with a few new twists. The Budapest mixes chicken livers, mushrooms, peas, and green paprika with spices for a lively choice. For dessert, the chestnut cream spiked with rum and decked in chocolate sauce and sugar is a sweet tooth's dream, and so is the crêpe starring pears cooked in red wine and served with cinnamon, chocolate, vanilla sauce, and a sprinkling of sugar.

I can't imagine coming here if you were not in the mood for a crêpe, but just in case, they do offer several soups, a small salad bar, grilled meats, and filled croissants. Wine, beer, and all spirits are also served.

TELEPHONE
317-4111
METRO
M3, Kálvin tér
OPEN
Daily
CLOSED
Never
HOURS
10 A.M.–10 P.M., continuous service
RESERVATIONS
Not necessary
CREDIT CARDS
None
À LA CARTE
500–1,100Ft
FIXED-PRICE MENU
None
SERVICE
Service discretionary
ENGLISH
Yes, and menu in English
MISCELLANEOUS
No-smoking section

(4) MÚZEUM
VIII. Múzeum körút 12

Around the corner from the National Museum is this Budapest institution, which has been drawing repeat customers since it opened in 1885. It is a dignified address where people come for a morning coffee and pastry, enjoy lunch before or after visiting the museum, and meet a friend for a glass of wine and perhaps stay on for dinner. All the fixtures in the room are original, including the sixteen wrought-iron-shaded chandeliers hanging from the high ceiling.

The menu is a good mix of Hungarian standards and tried-and-true international dishes.

TELEPHONE
338-4221
METRO
M3, Kálvin tér
OPEN
Mon–Sat
CLOSED
Sun
HOURS
10 A.M.–2 A.M., continuous service
RESERVATIONS
Suggested for dinner
CREDIT CARDS
AE
À LA CARTE
Coffee and pastry, 500–1,000Ft, meals, 1,700–3,000Ft, monthly special, 900–1,500Ft
FIXED-PRICE MENU
None
SERVICE
10% service added to the bill
ENGLISH
Yes, and menu in English

(5) RESTAURANT LÉGRÁDI & TSA $
V. Magyar u. 23

TELEPHONE
318-6804

METRO
M2, Astoria

OPEN
Mon–Sat dinner only

CLOSED
Sun

HOURS
6 P.M.–midnight

RESERVATIONS
Essential

CREDIT CARDS
AE, DC, MC, V

À LA CARTE
4,800–5,500Ft

FIXED-PRICE MENU
None

SERVICE
Service discretionary

ENGLISH
Yes, and menu in English

The wonderful thing for Cheap Eaters in Budapest is that Big Splurges rarely cost more than an average meal in any other European capital city. If you want a very special meal, then book ahead for one of the ten tables in this romantic and elegantly formal restaurant, which in the last century was the home of an eccentric baron. In 1987, it was the first privately owned restaurant to open in Budapest after the collapse of the Communist regime. From the street, you enter through an almost hidden, unobtrusive brown door and walk down a few steps to two intimate rooms, which have paintings of seventeenth- and eighteenth-century masters on the walls, Chippendale furniture, and tables set with Herend china and Berndorf silverware. A pianist and violinst add soft music to accompany the diners.

The Légrádi brothers' cuisine has a creative French international flair while remaining true to its Hungarian origins. I like to start with the asparagus cream soup or the caviar blini. The roasted quail on a bed of cabbage or the pork filet mignon stuffed with goose liver are richly rewarding main courses. If you like fish, order the fresh pike-perch, a delicate white fish from Lake Balaton, the largest lake in western and central Europe. The most sophisticated dessert is the orange soufflé with Grand Marnier sauce, but the more typical one is the creamy apricot pudding.

(6) SZENDVICS
VI. Bajcsy Zsilinsky út 7

TELEPHONE
Not available

METRO
All lines, Deák Ferenc tér

OPEN
Mon–Sat

CLOSED
Sun, holidays

HOURS
Mon–Fri 8 A.M.–6 P.M., Sat 9 A.M.–1 P.M., continuous service

RESERVATIONS
Not accepted

CREDIT CARDS
None

À LA CARTE
Sandwiches 60–80Ft

FIXED-PRICE MENU
None

SERVICE
No service charged or expected

ENGLISH
No, but not needed

Located next to a tacky tourist shop, "Sandwiches" is a gold mine that's busy all day long dispensing open-face sandwiches and pizza slices to the multitudes who pass by on their way to and from Deák Ferenc tér, Budapest's major metro hub where all three lines converge.

Fifteen or more varieties are on display, and you need only be guided by your eye and your level of hunger. Cost isn't much of a factor when you consider that if you spent all of $2, you could have four sandwiches—caviar, roast beef, fish, and pepperoni—and still walk out the door with some change.

(7) SZÁZÉVES ÉTTEREM RESTAURANT $
V. Pesti Barnabás u. 2

The Százéves Étterem Restaurant, on the ground floor of a Baroque palace, is the oldest restaurant in Budapest, and it is one of the most popular with visitors. In the evening, guests dine by candlelight and are accompanied by gypsy violinists. In the summer, there is a delightful terrace. The inside is rustic, with cushioned wooden booths and a stained-glass window defining the back wall.

House special appetizers include a savory strudel with bacon, mushrooms, and paprika, crêpes filled with veal and draped in a paprika cream sauce, and wild game pancakes in a wine and cranberry sauce. Meat eaters will be very happy with sirloin of beef cooked in "bull's blood" (Hungarian red wine), tournedos *kedvessy* style (tantalizingly prepared with mushrooms), goose liver, and the haunch of venison in red wine with ham, apples, and mushrooms and garnished with potato croquettes, rice, and vegetables. Vegetarians may want to seek other dinner arrangements. The dessert to die for—and you could, considering the fat grams—is the trio of white, chocolate, and nut sponge cakes served with vanilla ice cream, chocolate sauce, and whipped cream. As the waiter said when he brought it to the table, "Two thousand calories included, and very nice." How true.

TELEPHONE
318-3608

METRO
M3, Ferenciek tere

OPEN
Daily

CLOSED
Dec 24

HOURS
11 A.M.–midnight, continuous service

RESERVATIONS
Suggested for dinner

CREDIT CARDS
AE, DC, MC, V

À LA CARTE
5,500–6,000Ft

FIXED-PRICE MENU
None

SERVICE
Service discretionary

ENGLISH
Yes, and menu in English

(8) VEGETÁRIUM
V. Cukor u. 3

Jó étvágyat kivánunk! "We wish you a hearty appetite!" states the menu at this centrally located vegetarian restaurant. The restaurant says that the dishes are prepared in accordance with dietetic principles and that they represent a middle course between macrobiotic, vegan, reform, and raw form disciplines. It also claims that "If eaten regularly, our dishes will have a beneficial effect on health; some will have therapeutic value." The food is prepared with cold-pressed oils, sea salt, spring water, honey, and organic products when possible.

The menu changes several times a year and covers the vegetarian map from soups to main courses; it includes biological and Hungarian wines, alcohol-free beer, and assorted vegetable juices. Order just a bowl of soup to eat along with their delicious dark bread, or settle in for a full-course meal starting with goulash soup made with soy or sushi composed of nori algae stuffed with orange

TELEPHONE
267-0322

METRO
M3, Ferenciek tere

OPEN
Daily

CLOSED
Dec 24–25, Jan 1

HOURS
Noon–11:30 P.M., continuous service

RESERVATIONS
Suggested for dinner

CREDIT CARDS
AE, DC, MC, V

À LA CARTE
1,500–2,700Ft

FIXED-PRICE MENU
None

SERVICE
10% service added to bill

ENGLISH
Yes, and menu in English
MISCELLANEOUS
10% discount for students
No smoking allowed

and sweet-and-sour rice. Follow with the *cárpátian borzaska* (soy slivers served with garlic, sour cream, cheese, and brown rice) or the *meal of good haus:* potato flan with red wine soy ragout and paprika sauce. Tofu fixed several ways, pilafs, and Indian rice dishes, along with tempura vegetables, are other good choices. I'm not so sure about the *seitan vőneki,* a potato dish that comes with dried prunes and grilled ewe cheese, but you have to admit it is different.

The rustic basement room is brightened by butterfly painted walls and three fish tanks. Seating is around bare wood tables or at booths set with cork mats and paper napkins. In the evening there is classical guitar music, and there is a no-smoking policy in force at all times.

Cafés and Pastry Shops

(9) GERBEAUD CUKRÁSZDA
V. Vörösmarty tér 7

TELEPHONE
318-1311
METRO
M1, Vörösmarty tér
OPEN
Daily
CLOSED
Christmas Eve
HOURS
9 A.M.–9 P.M., continuous service
RESERVATIONS
Not necessary
CREDIT CARDS
AE, DC, MC, V
À LA CARTE
500–2,000Ft
FIXED-PRICE MENU
None
SERVICE
Service discretionary
ENGLISH
Yes

Gerbeaud, the most elegant and nostalgic coffee and pastry house in Budapest, has been on this site on Vörösmarty Square since Henrik Kugler opened it in 1858. It was sold in 1884 to Emil Gerbeaud, who created the famous Hungarian specialty *konyakos meggy*—a dark chocolate bonbon with a cognac-soaked cherry inside. The beautiful nineteenth-century decoration and furniture has been carefully preserved, attracting everyone, including most tourists who pass through the city. Still, it is a must-stop where you can choose from the largest selection of pastries in Budapest, order a light lunch, and buy their chocolate candies in packages stamped with the Kugler name.

Between the Inner and Outer Ring in Central Pest

This section of Budapest contains the Parliament; many government buildings, banks, and embassies; the theater district; Erzsébetváros (Elizabeth Town), which is the Jewish Quarter; and finally, Jozsefváros (south of Erzsébetváros), which is a run-down area known for prostitution, pornography, and other seamy sides of life.

RESTAURANTS

CAFÉS AND PASTRY SHOPS

A dollar sign ($) indicates a Big Splurge.

Restaurants

(10) FÉSZEK
VII. Kertész u. 36

The building once housed a monestary and a college for women, but for the past twenty years it has been home to Fészek, a restaurant specializing in wild game and fresh fish. When you first arrive, don't be put off by the drab exterior. The corner site looks deserted from the street, but once past the door and the two sets of hanging blankets (hung in the winter to keep out the cold), you enter a pleasant reception area with two nude statues and a chandelier. The restaurant itself, seating about 150, has curved ceilings and yellowing walls. In the summer, the 300-seat garden is where you want to be . . . and so

TELEPHONE
322-6043

METRO
M1, Oktogon

OPEN
Daily

CLOSED
Dec 24–25

HOURS
Noon–1 A.M., continuous service

RESERVATIONS
Suggested; essential for summer garden

CREDIT CARDS
AE, DC, MC, V

À LA CARTE
1,500–2,000Ft

FIXED-PRICE MENU
Lunch and dinner, 1,040Ft, 3 courses

SERVICE
Service discretionary

ENGLISH
Sometimes, but menu in English

does the rest of Budapest, so be sure to reserve ahead. Best Cheap Eating bets are the several fixed-price menus that offer a soup to start, two or three main-course selections, and a dessert. Unfortunately, the fixed-price menus do not offer wild game or fresh fish; you have to dine à la carte for these, but be careful, as the English à la carte menu does not list the prices.

NOTE: Kispipa Vendéglő, page 146, is under the same ownership.

(11) GRIFF ÉTTEREM
VII. Ákácfa u. 24

TELEPHONE
269-6664

METRO
M2, Blaha Lujza tér

OPEN
Mon–Fri dinner only, Sat lunch and dinner

CLOSED
Sun, holidays

HOURS
Mon–Fri 5 P.M.–midnight, Sat noon–midnight

RESERVATIONS
Suggested for dinner

CREDIT CARDS
AE, DC, MC, V

À LA CARTE
1,500–2,800Ft

FIXED-PRICE MENU
None

SERVICE
Service discretionary

ENGLISH
Yes, and menu in English

The theme of the Griff Étterem is the griffin, a mythological half-eagle, half-lion creature, and there are two griffin statues on the bar, another in full wingspan mounted over it, and yet another on the brass-and-copper coffee machine. The upstairs room has four formally set dark green velvet booths. Downstairs seats an additional thirty diners in a mirrored room that seems better geared for small groups than tables for two or four. The menu lists all the familiar Hungarian adaptations of beef and pork, but the real reason to try the Griff is its imaginative vegetarian menu. You can begin with a honey carrot salad or a bowl of garlic cream or Tokay wine soup. I like the sesame broccoli with ginger corn or the vegetable strudel with a parsley sauce as a main course. And for dessert . . . the house specialty, a rich cream-based pudding topped with a cinnamon vanilla sauce.

(12) KÁDÁR ÉTKEZDE
VII. Klauzál tér 9

TELEPHONE
321-3622

METRO
M2, Astoria or Blaha Lujza tér

OPEN
Tues–Sat lunch only

CLOSED
Sun–Mon, holidays

HOURS
11:30 A.M.–3:00 P.M.

RESERVATIONS
Not necessary

CREDIT CARDS
None

No one speaks English here, and the short menu is in Hungarian, but just look around at what your fellow diners are having and do as my friend's husband does wherever he is in the world—simply point and say, "I'll have what he/she is having." Amazingly enough, it always turns out to be something good.

Situated in the Jewish Quarter—and next to an interesting local market you should take the time to wander through—this legendary lunchroom represents a piece of Budapest's past. The half-paneled knotty pine room is plastered with signed photos of famous entertainers who have eaten here. The friendly owner, Gerami, stands by the blanket-draped door at a narrow table with a cash box and greets the regulars, who come for his wonderful soups and Jewish specials served on Friday. Be prepared to share your blue or red table, which is topped with plastic, a bread basket, a seltzer bottle, and plates holding the utensils and a paper napkin.

À LA CARTE
400–700Ft

FIXED-PRICE MENU
None

SERVICE
No service charged or expected

ENGLISH
Not much

(13) KÉTBALLÁBAS SÖRÖZŐ-ÉTTEREM $
VI. Terez körút 36, entrance on Dessewffy u. 61

The minute you walk in the door of this basement restaurant you know you are in soccer territory. The owner, George Bognár, played center for ten years on the Hungarian National Soccer Team. Now retired as a player, he is the trainer/manager of the BVSC Soccer Club. All around the room hang pictures of his team and of other well-known soccer players, managers, and trainers. His restaurant is just enough out of the way to keep it from being touristy. In fact, he firmly states that there are no gypsy violinists allowed.

The menu has French overtones and is too long for everything to be fresh. You can't tell me that wild hog stew or escargots served in Budapest are fresh! Nevermind, order a bottle of Hungarian wine, stick with the waiter's suggestions, and you will be content. I like the filling lamb ragout soup flavored with tarragon and the fillet steak, Hungarian style, covered with tomatoes and peppers. The Fogas fish from Lake Balaton, served in a shrimp, dill, and mushroom sauce, is another solid main-course choice. For a nice ending, the light sponge cake dumplings with chocolate sauce and whipped cream will keep you swearing off your diet for another day.

TELEPHONE
269-5563

METRO
M3, Nyugati pályaudvar, or M1, Oktogon

OPEN
Daily

CLOSED
Major holidays

HOURS
Noon–midnight, continuous service

RESERVATIONS
Advised for dinner

CREDIT CARDS
AE, DC, MC, V

À LA CARTE
2,500–3,800Ft

FIXED-PRICE MENU
None

SERVICE
Service discretionary

ENGLISH
Yes, and menu in English

(14) KISHARANG ÉTKEZDE
V. Október 6. u. 17

For a Cheap Eat in the heart of Budapest, you will be hard-pressed to top this local favorite, where no booze is served, no smoking is allowed, and prices are definitely not up with the times. It is a small place, with three shared tables and the kitchen in the back behind the cash register and the drink machines. Old cooking pots and implements hang on the walls along with an old clock and an assortment of seltzer bottles.

Hungarians are not noted for dainty appetites, small servings, or light cuisine. Cheap Eaters in Budapest will therefore appreciate not only the smaller portions

TELEPHONE
318-663

METRO
All lines, Deák Ferenc tér

OPEN
Daily; Sat–Sun lunch only

CLOSED
Major holidays

HOURS
Mon–Fri 11:30 A.M.–8 P.M., Sat–Sun 11:30 A.M.–4:30 P.M., continuous service

RESERVATIONS
Not necessary

CREDIT CARDS
Not accepted

À LA CARTE
Small portion 400–700Ft,
regular portion 725–1,000Ft

FIXED-PRICE MENU
None

SERVICE
10% service added to bill

ENGLISH
Limited, but menu in English

MISCELLANEOUS
No smoking allowed

available for almost everything on the menu, with the exception of the chef's specials and desserts, but the almost half-price tabs that are charged. If you ordered full servings of soup, a main course, salad, and dessert, you couldn't spend $10. If you order just half portions, it barely adds up to $3 or $4. What do you get for this phenomenal Cheap Eat? Nothing gourmet, that's for sure, but you will have a sturdy meal that should stick to your ribs for some time. Start with liver dumpling soup, followed by stuffed cabbage, beef goulash, macaroni, fried mushrooms, cheese, or pork, and then have a salad of cucumbers or peppers in vinegar. For dessert, it's either noodles with stewed cabbage or golden sweet dumplings. Ordering your meal to go costs an additional 25Ft (about 15¢).

(15) KISPIPA VENDÉGLŐ
VII. Ákácfa u. 38

TELEPHONE
342-2587

METRO
M2, Blaha Lujza tér

OPEN
Mon–Sat

CLOSED
Sun, holidays

HOURS
Noon–midnight, continuous
service

RESERVATIONS
Advised for lunch, essential for
dinner

CREDIT CARDS
AE, MC, V

À LA CARTE
1,200–2,500Ft

FIXED-PRICE MENU
Lunch and dinner, 900–
1,500Ft, 3 courses, no choices

SERVICE
Service discretionary

ENGLISH
Yes, and menu in English

Before the collapse of Communism in Hungary, Kispipa Vendéglő, which means "little pipe," was one of the few privately owned restaurants in Budapest. It has survived all the changes that have taken place since, and it remains very popular with the natives. The owner, Ervin Aubel, is always present to greet, serve, and make sure that everyone is being cared for properly. Despite several attempts at redecorating, the restaurant always looks the same, with bright lights, poster-covered walls, and cocoa brown tablecloths.

The menu is so extensive it is hard to imagine not finding something of interest, yet the chef will accommodate special requests whenever possible. Cheap Eaters will do well with any of the set-priced meals, and you certainly should pay attention to the daily printed menu, which changes with market availability. In the winter months, skip the plebian consommé in favor of the snail soup or the soothing game meat soup with quail eggs. Several hearty choices are the venison stew with red wine and the three rustic dishes made with wild hare. Pleasantly heavy endings include the Hungarian favorite of pancakes stuffed with curd or the chestnut püré with cream.

(16) LA FONTAINE $
V. Merlég u. 10

For a Cheap Eat taste of France in Budapest, La Fontaine is as close as it gets. The inside is a replica of a Parisian bistro, from the imported furniture and the cream-colored paper overlays on the tables to the nonchalant waiters draped in long white aprons. The lunch menus change weekly, and there are always daily specials written on the blackboard. The same à la carte menu served at dinner is available at lunch—when it has lower prices but fewer selections. The food isn't terribly creative, but it is a pleasant alternative to the heavy Hungarian cooking you encounter everywhere. You can start with either a salad, foie gras, or smoked salmon. The two main-course fish dishes are served with a choice of five sauces: white wine, caper, mushroom, saffron, or anis. The three meats—chicken, pork, or beef—come with your choice of eleven different sauces, including cognac, gin, whiskey, honey, and roquefort. *Tarte maison,* crème caramel, or a selection of cheese wrap it all up for lunch. For dinner you have the added option of chocolate mousse.

TELEPHONE
317-3715

METRO
M1, Bajcsy Zsilinszky út

OPEN
Mon–Sat

CLOSED
Sun, holidays

HOURS
Bar, noon–midnight; lunch noon–3 P.M., dinner 6 P.M.–midnight

RESERVATIONS
Not necessary

CREDIT CARDS
MC, V (8,000Ft minimum)

À LA CARTE
Lunch from 2,500Ft, dinner from 3,500Ft

FIXED-PRICE MENU
Lunch only, 1,100–1,400Ft, 2 courses, 1,200–1,500Ft, 3 courses, no choices

SERVICE
Service discretionary

ENGLISH
Yes, and French

(17) MIRTUSZ
VI. Jokai u. 8, corner Zichy Jenő u. 47

Mirtusz is a vegetarian restaurant with eight or so candle-lit tables sitting in an old arched cellar. Mirrors give the room depth, which has a fireplace at one end and botanical prints on the walls. Classical music in the background lends a quiet, calming air.

The biological wine list is carefully explained, as are the health benefits of many of the dishes and teas offered on the menu. For instance, you are informed that the dishes containing seaweed are helpful in detoxifying the body, and those with millet have an alkaline reaction that has a wholesome effect on skin, teeth, and bones. The lion's tooth tea is a blood purifyer, and thyme tea stimulates the brain. Luckily, the dishes are as good to eat as they are for you. The dishes are based on homey recipes as well as vegetarian preparations from around the world. Cream of wild mushroom (or hermit's) soup and a cream of kale soup with nutmeg are two imaginative winter starters. Six salads, fried lentil pâté, vegetables with various dips, or a mushroom pancake can serve as either heftier appetizers or light dishes. There

TELEPHONE
331-5920

METRO
M1, Oktogon

OPEN
Daily

CLOSED
Major holidays

HOURS
Noon–midnight, continuous service

RESERVATIONS
Not necessary

CREDIT CARDS
MC, V

À LA CARTE
Soups 300–350Ft, large salads 300–400Ft, one-dish meals 600–800Ft, 3 courses 1,100–1,400Ft

SERVICE
Service discretionary

ENGLISH
Yes, and menu in English

are at least a dozen main courses, with choices ranging from a mixed vegetable tempura to tofu in sesame sauce with vegetable croquettes and pasta with mushrooms or garlic.

(18) SVEJK RESTAURANT
VII. Király u. 59b (corner of Kurt u.)

TELEPHONE
322-3278
METRO
M1, Oktogon
OPEN
Daily
CLOSED
Never
HOURS
Noon–11 P.M., continuous service; live music 6–11 P.M.
RESERVATIONS
Not necessary
CREDIT CARDS
AE, DC, MC, V
À LA CARTE
1,800–2,400Ft
FIXED-PRICE MENU
None
SERVICE
Service discretionary
ENGLISH
Not much, but menu in English

The restaurant is named after Švejk, the Czech folk hero depicted in Jaroslav Hašek's famous stories (for a description of Švejk, see U Kalicha in Prague, page 54), and it emphasizes Czech food and beer. The interior of the beer hall–style restaurant has stone floors, scattered booths, high ladder-back chairs, and drawings on the walls that depict important moments in Švejk's life. The Czech beers include Pilsner Urquel, Budweiser, and six or seven other national brews.

The Bohemian dishes of note are the Slovak cabbage soup, made with sour cabbage, ham, sausage, and mushrooms; *straptaschka,* roast pork with ewe cheese–covered gnocchi; goulash à la Pilsen with bread dumplings; and for dessert, *csalafinta palacsinta*—crêpes with cherries.

(19) SZERB VENDÉGLŐ
V. Nagy Ignác u. 16

TELEPHONE
269-3139
METRO
M3, Nyugati pályaudvar
OPEN
Daily
CLOSED
Major holidays
HOURS
Mon–Sat 10 A.M.–11 P.M., Sun 10 A.M.–6 P.M., lunch menu 11 A.M.–3 P.M.
RESERVATIONS
Not necessary
CREDIT CARDS
MC, V
À LA CARTE
1,000–1,600Ft
FIXED-PRICE MENU
Lunch, 475Ft, 3 courses
SERVICE
Service discretionary
ENGLISH
Some

You will find Szerb Vendéglő not too far off Szent István körút, in a neighborhood not known for anything on the tourist map. If you have trouble spotting it, just look for the Gosser beer sign and the lamp by the door. The wood-paneled room is welcoming, with green floral-print tablecloths and rustic wooden chairs. Of course, there is nothing on the menu that is kind to your waistline, but the country-style cooking is served in belt-popping portions to a contented local crowd who don't seem to mind.

All the usual dishes are here, from goulash and paprika chicken to fried everything—from pig and goose liver to cheese and mushrooms. If you have any room left, rich pancakes with walnuts, poppyseeds, or jam for dessert will take care of it handily.

(20) TÜKÖRY SÖRÖZŐ
V. Hold u. 15

This restaurant serves Hungarian home cooking to bank clerks and businesspeople at lunch and to neighborhood Cheap Eaters in the evenings. At lunchtime you need a shoehorn to get in, even at 2 P.M., when people are still standing in the aisles waiting for a table to open up. With some luck, you will nab one of the booths that ring the room. Otherwise, you dine at communal tables in the middle of the room. The decor is not much, just some reproduction paintings slapped on the walls. But the food is good, and there's plenty of it.

If you like pork, you are in heaven, for they fix it here twelve different ways, from the simple to the confused. You can have it sliced, breaded, and fried, served as a stew over noodles, stuffed with sauerkraut and cabbage, or stuffed with mincemeat and mushrooms and cooked in a paprika sauce. A handful of beef dishes, liver fried three ways, a delicious smoked sausage soup served with a poached egg and sour cream, and the usual beet or cabbage salads round out the menu. The six desserts put the "h" on heavy . . . especially the curd dumplings covered with bread crumbs, fried in butter, and served with sour cream and your choice of salt or butter. Skip the wine this time and order a glass of Dreher, the Hungarian draught beer that goes so well with this type of meal.

NOTE: If you decide to brave the lunch crowd, stroll through the produce market next door. It is an interesting example of what is available to the average resident in Budapest. Anytime you are here, you can't fail to admire the unusually ornate bank building across the street.

TELEPHONE
269-5027, 331-1931

METRO
M3, Arany Janus utca

OPEN
Mon–Fri

CLOSED
Sat–Sun, holidays

HOURS
10 A.M.–midnight, continuous service

RESERVATIONS
Not accepted

CREDIT CARDS
MC, V

À LA CARTE
600–1,000Ft

FIXED-PRICE MENU
Lunch only, 380Ft, 3 courses, several choices

SERVICE
Service discretionary

ENGLISH
Limited, but menu in English

Cafés and Pastry Shops

(21) CAFÉ MOZART
VII. Erzsébet körút 36

If you like Viennese coffee and pastries, or ice cream fantasy sundaes, Café Mozart is for you. It is a bit schmaltzy, with costumed waitresses serving diners in two pink rooms that are frankly feminine, but there is no argument about the quality of the pastries or the ice cream. The menu starts with a listing of over eighty coffees, all painstakingly described, from a simple espresso to the quartet spiked with various liqueurs. The

TELEPHONE
352-0664

METRO
M1, Oktogon

OPEN
Daily

CLOSED
Never

HOURS
9 A.M.–11 P.M.

RESERVATIONS
Not accepted

CREDIT CARDS
Not accepted

À LA CARTE
Coffee 175–850Ft, pastries
140–400Ft, ice cream 300–
900Ft

FIXED-PRICE MENU
None

SERVICE
Service discretionary

ENGLISH
Some, and menu in English

same goes for the pastry possibilities, which take up twelve pages of the menu, tempting you with apple strudel, lemon cream cake, truffle torte, and Strauss carrot cake. If this isn't enough, keep going to the ice cream section, which uses "the finest Bob and Rob American style ice cream." I don't know what brand they are talking about, only that it is mighty good. You could go easy and just have a single scoop with whipped cream, but how dull when you could dip into the Salzburg, which tops scoops of chocolate chip and rum raisin ice creams with chocolate sauce, whipped cream, and chocolate candy. Then there's the Gloriette: a whole banana with chocolate, rum raisin, and carmel ice creams topped with pineapple, chocolate, caramel, whipped cream, and a cookie. Don't even mention that four-letter "d" word.

(22) MŰVÉSZ KÁVÉHÁZ
VI. Andrássy út 29

TELEPHONE
267-0289

METRO
M1, Opera

OPEN
Mon–Sat

CLOSED
Sun

HOURS
8 A.M.–10 P.M.

RESERVATIONS
Not necessary

CREDIT CARDS
Not accepted

Á LA CARTE
Coffee 160–400Ft, pastries
100–250Ft

FIXED-PRICE MENU
None

SERVICE
Service discretionary

ENGLISH
Yes

On Pest's main boulevard, almost opposite the Opera, the Művész Kávéház is one of the few remaining turn-of-the-century coffeehouses in the city. The name means "artist," and you still might spot one or two around the room, along with die-hard regulars, little old ladies, and the occasional corporate-type. The building was fortunately saved from extinction a few years ago, and the beautiful interior is untouched and intact. Also untouched are the sagging seats with springs that wore out years ago. The menu is simple and simply approached: forget the open-face sandwiches and order a pastry and coffee.

(23) NEW YORK KÁVÉHÁZ
VII. Erzsébet körút 9–11

TELEPHONE
322-3849, 322-1648

METRO
M2, Blaha Lujza tér

OPEN
Daily

CLOSED
Dec 24, sometimes for private
parties

Some say it is the most beautiful coffeehouse in the world. It certainly is the most beautiful in Budapest, but *only* from the inside. The outside is a crumbling wreck held up by scaffolding installed in 1956 after a Soviet tank rammed the building. The deterioration of the exterior has progressed to the point where it may not be repairable. If so, that would be a tragedy. The building was built in 1896 by the New York Insurance Company, who wanted to show the world how rich and successful it was. Construction took seven years. When it finally opened, most of the building's occupants were publishing companies, and it wasn't long before the magnificent Art Nouveau coffeehouse became the literary and artistic heart of Budapest.

Years of neglect, and a ten-year period when the entire building lay empty, took its toll, but the interior has now been restored to its past splendor and glory. However, under the Communist regime, the many crystal chandeliers were removed and apparently destroyed, only to be replaced by 760 of the ugliest modern globe lights imaginable. Today, no one comes to New York Kávéház to eat. The food is mediocre and overpriced. People come instead for a coffee and to sit for awhile admiring this sad reminder of Budapest's vibrant past.

HOURS
Noon–midnight

RESERVATIONS
Not necessary

CREDIT CARDS
AE, DC, MC, V

À LA CARTE
Coffee and pastry 500–800Ft

FIXED-PRICE MENU
None

SERVICE
250Ft cover, service discretionary

ENGLISH
Yes

Beyond the Outer Ring

RESTAURANTS

CAFÉS AND PASTRY SHOPS

A dollar sign ($) indicates a Big Splurge.

Restaurants

(24) BAGOLYVÁR $
XIV. Állatkerti út 2

Gundel, a restaurant founded in the early 1900s by the great Hungarian chef Károly Gundel, is once again Budapest's most famous place to dine; it is recognized throughout Europe for its elegant interior and masterful cuisine. In 1992, Ronald Lauder, former U.S. ambassador to Hungary, and George Lang, the well-known Hungarian-American restaurateur, took it over and spent millions to restore it in sumptuous Art Nouveau style. As you can imagine, the food served in this culinary temple does not embody the spirit of a book entitled *Cheap Eats.* You can, however, sample George Lang's

TELEPHONE
351-6395, 343-0217

METRO
M1, Hősök tere

OPEN
Daily

CLOSED
Never

HOURS
Noon–11 P.M., continuous service

RESERVATIONS
Essential

CREDIT CARDS
AE, DC, MC, V

À LA CARTE
2,200–4,000Ft

FIXED-PRICE MENU
Lunch only, 2,100Ft, 3 courses,
no choices

SERVICE
Service discretionary

ENGLISH
Yes, and menu in English

noted cuisine in what is known as his budget, or junior, Grundel, at the Transylvanian castle lodge called Bagolyvár (which means Owl Palace), located just around the corner.

Rest assured, you are not settling for second best by reserving a table at Bagolyvár. Because it is close to Városliget—Budapest's largest park, which contains a zoo, circus, outdoor winter ice skating rink, Vajdahunyad Castle, an old-fashioned amusement park, and thermal baths—it is a very popular choice, especially for Sunday family outings. As you enter, you are ushered into a sitting area with framed black-and-white photos of Hungarian families celebrating weddings, christenings, birthdays, and other rights of passage. To one side is an open window onto part of the kitchen and a corner display of the restaurant's wines and jams and George Lang's cookbooks for sale. The large, open dining room has a semipitched roof, formally set tables, and two summer terraces.

The food celebrates the homespun goodness of Hungarian village cooking. The fixed-price lunch menu features wild game in the winter. If you order à la carte, you are faced with choosing between roast veal, pan-braised goose leg, or skewered beef, turkey, and pork. Potato salad with Spanish onions, pickled green peppers, or fresh beets are only three of the varying side dishes. For dessert, the walnut-, cheese-, or jam-filled pancakes covered with chocolate sauce are a delicious reminder that no one takes dieting seriously in Budapest.

Cafés and Pastry Shops

(25) LUKÁCS CUKRÁSZDA
VI. Andrássy út 70

Located on a wide boulevard housing many embassy residences and international company offices, Lukács Cukrászda is a pleasant stop if you are visiting Budapest's largest park, Városliget (see description above under Bagolyvár). There is a pastry display as you enter, and the formal brocaded room has gold-trimmed walls, crystal chandeliers, and green marble-topped tables. In addition to the usual coffee, pastries, and ice cream, tea sandwiches and salads are served.

TELEPHONE
302-8747

METRO
M1, Bajza utca or Hősök tere

OPEN
Daily

CLOSED
Christmas, New Year's

HOURS
8 A.M.–9 P.M.

RESERVATIONS
Not necessary

CREDIT CARDS
Not accepted

À LA CARTE
Coffee 170–320Ft, pastries 120–220Ft, ice cream 400–500Ft

SERVICE
Service discretionary

ENGLISH
Limited, but menu is in English

BUDA

Buda, on the west side of the Danube, is as hilly as Pest is flat. Older than Pest, it is less commercial and more residential. The most visited sections are Castle Hill, Gellért Hill, and the area between the two along the Danube.

Castle Hill

The sweeping views and the imposing gothic Matthias Church make this the most beautiful part of Budapest. Hardy souls will enjoy walking along the steep pathways and narrow lanes that lead to it. Others can take a shuttle bus from Moszkva tér, or the funicular from Clark Adam tér. The only business on the hill is tourism.

RESTAURANTS

CAFÉS AND PASTRY SHOPS

A dollar sign ($) indicates a Big Splurge.

Restaurants

TELEPHONE
None

METRO
All lines, Deák Ferenc tér, then bus No. 16; or M2, Moszkva tér, then the Várbusz bus, which goes directly to Castle Hill

OPEN
Mon–Fri lunch only

CLOSED
Sat–Sun, holidays

HOURS
11:30 A.M.–2:30 P.M.

RESERVATIONS
Not accepted

CREDIT CARDS
Not accepted

À LA CARTE
300–600Ft

SERVICE
No service charged or expected

ENGLISH
None, but you won't need it

(26) AKADÉMIA ÖNKISZOLGÁLO ÉTTEREM
I. Országház u. 3

This Cheap Eat, lunch-only cafeteria is definitely nothing special or gourmet, but it is cheap and filling, and even though it's across the street from the Hilton Hotel, few tourists or foreigners ever stumble across it. Just as you enter the Fortuna Passage, walk past the first restaurant door on your left and go into the second, which is a stairway leading up to the cafeteria. Hang your coat on one of the hooks lining the entry, get in line, grab a tray and some silverware, and join the chow line. Then take your food to one of the tables in the big dining room with red carpeted stages. Your dining companions will be old ladies, pensioners, workers in overalls, shopkeepers, and assorted others who know a good meal deal when they find it.

(27) PEST-BUDA $
I. Fortuna u. 3

The name of the restaurant goes back to the days when Buda and Pest were two distinctly different towns. Black-and-white prints of old Budapest remind you of that past, and so does the interesting collection of hundred-year-old menus and the glass display case of antique restaurant utensils, china, and other relics on loan from the Catering Museum across the street.

The house specialties are goulash soup, pheasant soup spiked with Tokay wine, grilled pike-perch with cray-fish, and "drunken steak," which is flavored with cognac and served with apricots, mushrooms, and potato croquets. Pork chops stuffed with duck liver are given a Hungarian twist with the addition of tomatoes and paprika. Sweet dessert dumplings swimming in vanilla and chocolate sauce, not to mention whipped cream, keep wayward waistlines expanding another notch.

TELEPHONE
212-5880
METRO
All lines, Deák Ferenc tér, then bus No. 16; or M2, Moszkva tér, then the Várbusz bus, which goes directly to Castle Hill
OPEN
Daily
CLOSED
Never
HOURS
Noon–midnight, continuous service
RESERVATIONS
Suggested for dinner
CREDIT CARDS
MC, V
À LA CARTE
3,200–4,000Ft
FIXED-PRICE MENU
Lunch and dinner, 3,000Ft and 3,800Ft, 3 courses, no choices
SERVICE
Service discretionary
ENGLISH
Yes, and menu in English

Cafés and Pastry Shops

(28) RUSZWURM CUKRÁSZDA
I. Szentháromság u. 7

All business on Castle Hill is conducted primarily for tourists, and you will not be able to escape the hype. At this dignified, quiet, and very pleasant tearoom, you can at least order a steaming cup of tea, coffee, or hot choco-late along with one of their famous cream-filled pastries and enjoy the Empire-style furnishings and antique toys and boxes lining the room. All the food is made in the little kitchen in the back, and it is delicious—and defi-nitely worth the wait you will surely encounter for a table.

TELEPHONE
375-5284
METRO
All lines, Deák Ferenc tér, then bus No. 16; or M2, Moszkva tér, then Várabusz to Castle Hill
OPEN
Daily
CLOSED
Christmas
HOURS
10 A.M.–7 P.M.
RESERVATIONS
Not necessary
CREDIT CARDS
Not accepted
À LA CARTE
Coffee from 100Ft, cakes 110–200Ft
FIXED-PRICE MENU
None
SERVICE
Service discretionary
ENGLISH
Yes

Between Castle Hill and Gellért Hill

The area between Castle Hill and Gellért Hill along Fő út is known as Viziváros, or Watertown. Farther along the Danube is an area of parks known as the Tabán area. When the Turks occupied Budapest, this area was filled with taverns, wine cellars, and houses of prostitution. For centuries, the crumbling neighborhood remained very poor and unsanitary, and finally in the early part of the twentieth century, it was declared uninhabitable and almost entirely razed. Today it is mainly green spaces.

RESTAURANTS

CAFÉS AND PASTRY SHOPS

Restaurants

(29) ARANYSZARVAS
I. Szarvas tér 1

TELEPHONE
375-6451

METRO
From Március 15 tér, on Pest side of Erzsébet híd, take bus No. 5 or 78

OPEN
Daily

CLOSED
Christmas

HOURS
Oct–May, Mon–Fri 4–11 P.M., Sat–Sun noon–11 P.M.; June–Sept, daily noon–11 P.M., continuous service; gypsy music Mon–Sat 7–11 P.M.

RESERVATIONS
Suggested, especially on weekends and for summer terrace

CREDIT CARDS
AE, DC, MC, V

À LA CARTE
2,500–2,800Ft

The Aranyszarvas restaurant occupies one of the few original buildings near Gellért Hill, and it is known for its preparation of wild game. The pleasant two-room interior stresses its hunting theme with stag horns mounted on the walls and fashioned into brass lights, and in the summer there is a pleasant terrace that seats eighty people. The cooking philosophy is summed up by a quote on the menu, which is taken from an eighteenth-century cookbook: "Game is a delicacy on the table because it is delicious, healthy and easy to digest. An expert cook can make it into the finest dishes of any cuisine."

This is an excellent restaurant for a particular type of diner: the dedicated carnivore and lover of wild game who is willing to experiment with some unusual offerings and preparations. Starting with the appetizers, try the wild boar pâté spiked with horseradish sauce or the pancakes with venison in a white wine sauce. Saddle of hare with bread dumplings is a special main course, as are any of the wild boar selections, either roasted and served with roquefort cheese and oranges, cut into fillets and topped with goose liver and mushrooms, or prepared in a red wine sauce. Larded pheasant, wild duck, and venison also receive equal billing. Dessert is the only game-free zone on the menu, but after such a feast, probably a Mária Theresa coffee spiked with cointreau and whipped cream will be about all you can manage.

FIXED-PRICE MENU
None
SERVICE
Service discretionary
ENGLISH
Yes, and menu in English

(30) HORGÁSZTANYA VENDÉGLŐ
I. Fő út 27

The name Horgásztanya means Angler's Hut, which is your first clue as to what's best on the menu. The fish theme is further carried out by the decidedly corny nautical decor: not only are there swagged fish nets but a boat hangs from the back wall along with a red-and-white life preserver. Surprisingly, the menu lists almost every fried version of beef, pork, and poultry plus a few wild game selections. Forget them all and stay focused on the seventeen fish dishes. You can enjoy carp made into soup, served with pasta, fried with a side of tartar sauce, or grilled and covered with a dill cream crab ragout. Catfish is also fried or grilled, and the trout almondine is cooked in butter. No one said the preparations would have a light touch—this *is* Budapest, after all, the home of heavy-handed cooking. However, these fish preparations do offer some respite from a totally meat-dominated diet.

TELEPHONE
201-0683
METRO
M2, Batthyány tér
OPEN
Daily
CLOSED
Major holidays
HOURS
Noon–midnight, continuous service
RESERVATIONS
Suggested for dinner
CREDIT CARDS
Not accepted
À LA CARTE
1,300–1,700Ft
FIXED-PRICE MENU
None
SERVICE
Service discretionary
ENGLISH
Yes, and menu in English

Cafés and Pastry Shops

(31) ANGELIKA
I. Batthyány tér 7

Next to the Baroque St. Anna Church on Batthyány Square and facing the Danube is one of Budapest's favorite coffeehouses. It has an old-fashioned air, with several comfortably fitted rooms laid out to encourage long talks with special people. One page of the menu lists the coffees and teas, while three are devoted to the housemade pastries, which tells you what is uppermost in the minds of most Budapest citizens.

TELEPHONE
201-4847
METRO
M2, Batthyány tér
OPEN
Daily
CLOSED
Major holidays
HOURS
10 A.M.–8 P.M.
RESERVATIONS
Not necessary
CREDIT CARDS
Not accepted
À LA CARTE
Coffee 170–800Ft, pastries 200–300Ft
FIXED-PRICE MENU
None
SERVICE
Service discretionary
ENGLISH
Limited, but menu in English

The Foot of the Buda Hills

Unless you have a car, or are a frequent visitor to Budapest, you probably won't venture very far into the Buda Hills. That is a shame, since this residential area has some lovely parts to it, as well as expensive hotels and good restaurants. The two listed below are plain-Jane neighborhood places where you will seldom run into another tourist, but you will get a good look at the local fauna and flora.

RESTAURANTS

Restaurants

(32) MÁJAS VENDÉGLŐ
XII. Kiss János altábornagy u. 38

TELEPHONE
312-3740

METRO
All lines, Deák Ferenc tér, then bus No. 105; or M2, Moszkva tér, then Tram No. 59

OPEN
Daily

CLOSED
Never

HOURS
8 A.M.–10 P.M., continuous service

RESERVATIONS
Not taken

CREDIT CARDS
Not accepted

À LA CARTE
800–1,000Ft

FIXED-PRICE MENU
None

SERVICE
Service discretionary

ENGLISH
Yes

Close to nothing I can think of, this corner restaurant in a blue-collar section of the Buda Hills is typical of hundreds just like it most tourists never see. The outside is hardly alluring—plastered as it is with bright red Coke signs—and decor doesn't get much better inside. The bar is held up by crusty regulars, and the few tables are usually filled like clockwork by locals who arrive at the same time each day.

The owner, who is also the chief cook and bottle washer, is a gentleman named Attila Száva. When I commented on his good English, he smiled and told me that he had worked at the Pensacola Yacht Club in Florida from 1991 to 1994 when he decided to return to his native country and open his own restaurant. It's a great story, and it gets even better when you taste his simple home cooking, which his customers eat and enjoy with complete abandon. When you go, look to see what he has written on the daily menu hanging on the wall. He selects whatever is fresh and appealing from the market, and changes the dishes daily. His sauerkraut soup, loaded with sausage, is the real thing, and so is the pork and veal stuffed cabbage. The dessert specialty is *somlói galuska,* a wonderful mixture of nuts and raisins rolled in pancakes and covered with vanilla cream and whipped cream. No, it's not destination dining, but for a taste of what the average Budapest citizen eats on a daily basis, you can't go wrong.

After your meal, walk around the neighborhood, which provides a look at Budapest living, which is certainly not lavish here. Walk along Beethoven utca until you cross Böszörményi út, and you will come to a children's playground.

(33) MAKKHETES VENDÉGLŐ
XII. Német Völgyi út 56

This is a good place to try for a Sunday lunch. No one speaks much English, since few English-speaking tourists ever wander this far. The building dates from the twenties, and it has a terrace that is used in the summer. Tables are set with the napkin and eating utensils sitting on the soup plate. When ordering, concentrate on the typed insert inside the regular menu; this features the specials of the day. The rich food, which is sustaining and geared toward the very hungry, ignores all dietary concerns. Good examples include thick goulash soup, goose liver risotto, and minced, spiced pork that's layered with rice and cabbage, covered with sour cream, then baked in the oven.

TELEPHONE
355-7330

METRO
All lines, Deák Ferenc tér, then bus No. 105

OPEN
Daily

CLOSED
Holidays

HOURS
11 A.M.–8 P.M., continuous service

RESERVATIONS
Not necessary

CREDIT CARDS
Not accepted

À LA CARTE
1,000–2,000Ft

FIXED-PRICE MENU
None

SERVICE
Service discretionary

ENGLISH
None, but menu in English

Glossary of Helpful Phrases and Menu Terms

Even Hungarians admit that, unless Hungarian is your mother tongue, mastering it is almost impossible and deciphering it only slightly less daunting. Fortunately for Cheap Eaters in Budapest, almost every restaurant has a multilingual menu for its regular dishes and someone on the staff who has at least a rudimentary command of English. However, in some of the smaller establishments, the daily specials are not translated. It is useful, therefore, to have a few basic words and phrases at your disposal.

General Phrases

Do you speak English?	*Beszél angolul?*
I do not speak Hungarian	*Nem beszélek Magyarul*
I do not understand	*Nem értem*
yes/no	*igen/nem*
Good day/Hello	*Jó napot*
Good evening	*Jó estét*
Goodbye	*Viszontlátásra*
Please/thank you	*Kérem/köszönöm*
You are welcome	*Islen hozott*
Excuse me	*Bocsánat*
good/bad	*jó/rossz*
open/closed	*nyitva/zárva*

Numbers

0	*nulla*
1	*egy*
2	*kettő*
3	*három*
4	*négy*
5	*öt*
6	*hat*
7	*hét*
8	*nyolc*
9	*kilenc*
10	*tíz*
11	*tizenegy*
12	*tizenkettő*
13	*tizenhárom*
14	*tizennégy*

15	*tizenöt*
16	*tizenhat*
17	*tizenhét*
18	*tizennyolc*
19	*tizenkilenc*
20	*húsz*
30	*harminc*
40	*negyven*
50	*ötven*
60	*hatvan*
70	*hetven*
80	*nyolcvan*
90	*kilencven*
100	*száz*
200	*kettőszáz*
300	*háromszáz*
1,000	*ezer*
10,000	*tizezer*

Days of the Week

Monday	*Hétfő*
Tuesday	*Kedd*
Wednesday	*Szerda*
Thursday	*Csütörtök*
Friday	*Péntek*
Saturday	*Szombat*
Sunday	*Vasárnap*

Eating Out

Bon Appetit!/Cheers!	*Jó étvágyat!/Egészségedre!*
breakfast	*reggeli*
lunch	*ebéd*
dinner	*vacsora*
I would like...	*Kérnék...*
a table	*egy asztalt*
a menu	*egy étlapot*
to pay	*fizetni szeretnék*
I am a vegetarian/diabetic	*Vegetáriánus vagyok/diabetikus vagyok*
I did not order this	*Én nem ezt rendeltem*
Do you have?	*Van?*
bill	*számla*
waiter/waitress	*pincér/kisasszony*
wine list	*itallap*
beverages	*italok*
cup	*csésze*
fork	*villa*

glass	*pohár*
knife	*kés*
napkin	*szalvetá*
plate	*tányér*
spoon	*kanál*

Basic Menu Terms

citrom	lemon
csipős	hot (spicy)
cukro	sugar
ecet	vinegar
előételek	appetizers
főetelek	main courses
forró	hot (temperature)
friss	fresh
híd eg	cold
kenyér/vaj	bread/butter
olaj	oil
só/bors	salt/pepper

Methods of Preparation

főzött	boiled
párolt	steamed
pörkölt	stew
sütve	baked, fried
jól átsütve	well-done
félig átsütve	rare
közepesen átsütve	medium

Meat (*husok*)

bárány	lamb
bécsi szelet	wienerschnitzel (breaded veal)
borjú	veal
gulyás	goulash
kolbász	sausage
marha	beef
máj	liver
sertés	pork
sonka	ham

Game (*vadételek*)

nyúl	rabbit
vaddisznó pörkölt	wild boar stew
szarvas	deer
őz	venison
őz ragut	venison stew

Poultry (baromfi)

csirke	chicken
kacsa	duck
liba	goose
mell	breast
pulyka	turkey

Fish/Seafood (halételek)

csuka	pike
fogas	pike-perch
halászlé	fish stew
homár	lobster
kagyló	shellfish/mussels
lazac	salmon
pisztráng	trout
ponty	carp
rak	crab
tonhal	tuna

Soups (levesek)

bajai halászlé	fish and potato soup
burgonya krémleves	cream of potato
erőleves/húsgombóccal	consommé/with meat balls
gombaleves	mushroom
gulyásleves	goulash
jókai bableves	bean soup with pork
paradicsomleves	tomato
spárga krémleves	cream of asparagus
zöldségleves	vegetable

Salads (saláták)

cékla	beetroot
fejes saláta	green salad
paprika saláta	picked-pepper salad
uborka saláta	cucumber salad
vitamin saláta	mixed salad with mayonnaise

Eggs (tojas)

buggyantott	poached
ételek	egg dishes
főtt	boiled
kemény	hard-boiled
lágy	soft-boiled
omlett	omelette
rántotta	scrambled
tükör	fried

Side Dishes *(köretek)*

galuska	dumplings/noodles
rizs	rice

Vegetables *(zöldség)*

babok	beans
burgonya/krumplí	potatoes
főtt	boiled
hasáb	fries
püré	mashed
sült	baked
fokhagyma	garlic
gomba	mushroom
hagyma	onion
káposzta	cabbage
karfiol	cauliflower
paprika	pepper (sweet)
paradicsom	tomatoes
sárgarépa	carrot
savanyúkáposzta	sauerkraut
spenót	spinach
zöldbab	green beans
zöldborsó	green peas

Fruit *(gyümölcs)*

alma	apple
barack	apricot
cseresznye	cherry
dinnye	melon
dió	walnut
eper	strawberries
gesztenye	chestnuts
körte	pear
meggy	sour cherry
narancs	orange
őszibarack	peach
szilva	plums
szőlő	grapes

Desserts *(desszertek)*

almas rétes	apple strudel
dobos torta	layered cake
fagylalt	ice cream
palacsinta	pancakes filled with fruit and/or ice cream and covered in chocolate sauce

somlói galuska	sponge cake soaked in cream, rum, and chocolate sauce
túrós rétes	cheese strudel

Drinks *(italok)*

ásványvíz	mineral water
borok	wine
édes	sweet
fehér	white
száraz	dry
vörös	red
gyümölcslé	fruit juice
jég	ice
kakaó	hot chocolate
kávé	coffee
fekete	black
koffeinmentes	decaffeinated
tejes	with milk
tejszines	with cream
koktél	cocktail
narancslé	orange juice
narancsszörp	orangeade
pezsgő	champagne
sör/barna/világos	beer/dark/lager
tej/meleg/híd eg	milk/hot/cold
unicum	bitter herbal liqueur
víz/forró/híd eg	water/hot/cold

Index of Restaurants

Readers' Comments

In *Cheap Eats in Prague, Vienna, and Budapest,* I recommend places as they were when I tried them and as this book went to press. While every effort has been made to ensure the accuracy of the information presented, the reader must understand that—especially in the rapidly changing restaurant picture in Prague and Budapest—prices, menu selections, opening and closing times, vacation schedules, and ownership can change overnight. Also remember that telephone numbers in Prague and Budapest will continue to change due to the privatization of the telephone systems. Therefore, the author and the publisher cannot accept responsibility for any changes that may be found.

Cheap Eats in Prague, Vienna, and Budapest is updated on a regular basis. If you find some place that has changed or make a discovery that you'd like to pass along, please send me a note stating the name and address of the restaurant, the date of your visit, and a description of your findings. Your comments are extremely important to me, and many ultimately lead to improving subsequent editions. As many readers already know, I read, answer, and follow through on every letter I receive. Thank you for taking the time to write.

Please send your letters to Sandra A. Gustafson, *Cheap Eats in Prague, Vienna, and Budapest,* c/o Chronicle Books, 85 Second St., Sixth Floor, San Francisco, CA 94105.